together with christ

Together with Christ

a dating couple's devotional

52 devotions and bible studies
to nurture your relationship

chelsea damon

ALTHEA
PRESS

To Josh, my favorite person to laugh and cry with.
You give me something I love writing about.

contents

how to use this book

Before I tell you how to use this book, I want to tell you why I wrote it in the first place.

My husband, Josh, and I got married after three years of dating. Our story is fairly typical: We were 18 years old and had just moved into brother-sister dorms at a Christian university in Lynchburg, Virginia. We met during a freshman orientation scavenger hunt, and a week or two later, we had our first date at a coffee shop. We were inseparable after that, for better or for worse.

Our engagement lasted four months, most of which we spent apart, since I had moved back in with my family in New Jersey and Josh had moved back in with his family in Washington State. Being apart, we didn't have the opportunity (or time) to seek out premarital counseling, so we skipped it. To make up for that, I read every marriage book I could in those four months. I was about to finally start what I had waited my whole life for, and for goodness' sake, I was going to get it right!

Equally yoked? Check.

Submission? Check.

Expectations? Check.

Conversations about family? Check.

We were ready! Right?

Now I want to say here that I knew Josh wasn't perfect (nobody is). But I did know that he loved God. And anyone who really loved God would be willing to be introspective and make changes as needed in order to make the relationship work, wouldn't they? Easier said than done. We were married for six months when we found out we were pregnant with our son. Combine that with trying to finish college, working part-time jobs to support our growing family, and having little to no support system, and it would be an understatement to say we had a rocky first couple of years.

During that time, God grew us and stretched us in ways we never imagined having to grow or be stretched. If I had married someone I wasn't *sure* could be introspective *and* who loved Christ, our marriage would likely have fallen apart. The thing is, you can't make someone be introspective, and you can't make someone love Jesus. What you can do is be introspective yourself, pray (a lot), confront sin when needed, show grace, and have hope that Christ will bring all things together for His glory in the end.

That's how I want you to use this book—as a tool to inspire your own introspection, with the hope that God will use this book and the Scripture you read alongside it to grow you into a more spiritually mature person who is ready to take on life with a partner.

This book is designed to be a weekly devotional. It has 52 chapters, one for each week of the year. Every Sunday night (or whichever day/ time works best for your schedules), sit down with your partner, pray together, read a chapter, and save a significant amount of time at the end for discussion, prayer, and journaling about what you're learning. Write down the areas in your life where you're struggling. You should also feel free to write about any areas where you would like to see change in your significant other, but don't leave it at that. Pray about those things, for yourself and your partner.

You may read something in these pages that makes you think, *This is totally something my significant other/fiancé(e)/spouse needs to work on. They do this all the time!* You're probably right! Your significant other probably does mess up. But even from the beginning of time, we can see that putting the blame on others comes way too easily: "The man said, 'The woman whom you gave to be with me, she gave me fruit of the tree, and I ate'" (Genesis 3:12).

I encourage you, before each and every time you sit down to read this book, whether alone or with someone else, to pray that God will open your eyes. Ask Him to reveal to you these three things:

- Areas of sin in your life that need to be dealt with

- Areas where you could grow more spiritually mature

- Areas where you can show grace toward others

If you do that, I promise this book will be much more useful to you than if you sit down with your significant other wondering what lesson *they're* going to learn today.

While this book is written with the idea that dating or engaged couples will read it together, it can also be read by singles, recently married people, or even groups. When you finish it, you can keep it around as a resource for topics that may come up at a later time, or you can simply begin it again. If you do begin it again, look back at your journal to remember what God was teaching you a year ago and compare it to what He is teaching you now.

As you read and pray through this book, know that I'm also praying for you. I pray that God will teach you new things, make Himself great in your life, and that your relationships will reflect His love and grace in your lives.

Open Communication

A soft answer turns away wrath, but a harsh word stirs up anger.

—

Proverbs 15:1

Over the course of my life, and especially my marriage, I've had the opportunity to speak to many individuals about their relationships. Often they'll ask me something like "What do you think they meant by that?" or "What should I say to them?"

Josh and I have long had extremely open communication in our relationship—but I haven't always functioned that way. Like many others, I used to wonder what people really meant when they said something I didn't understand, and I struggled to figure out how to convey what I meant without hurting someone's feelings or being misunderstood. Unfortunately, when people use this approach, they often leave important things unsaid or important questions unasked, for fear of being awkward or digging up something uncomfortable. I used to be terrible at handling conflict and confrontation for these very reasons.

My first experience with overcoming these fears came not in my relationship with Josh but when I shared an apartment with four other women in college, all of whom were very different and had different expectations of each other. Since I was the person who had orchestrated finding the apartment, locating roommates, splitting rent and utilities, and so on, I also found myself (whether I liked it or not) in the role of house mother. If there was a conflict, I often had to intervene in order to keep the peace.

During that year, I found one thing to be almost universally true: Asking clarifying questions almost never offends anyone (at least anyone who is mostly reasonable). I also found that explaining or even overexplaining myself and my reasoning tended not to offend anyone, either.

Here's an example of what that might look like: Let's say my roommates and I were having a discussion about laundry. I might ask, "So, do you think that if your laundry is left in the dryer, whoever needs to use the dryer next should fold it and put it away for you?" Then I'd wait for their response. If the answer was no, then we were all in agreement. If the answer was yes, then we had more talking to do, e.g., "I feel it would be fairer to everyone if we were all responsible for folding and putting away our own laundry."

This part is often the most difficult for anyone: making a statement that you know others disagree with. However, in being honest and sharing your true thoughts, you avoid more frustration than you cause. This is the same in any relationship, romantic or platonic. If Josh and I were having a disagreement about whose family to visit this weekend, I could hold my tongue and be frustrated, feeling that he's being selfish and not offering to take us to see my family. Or I could be open about my thoughts, share them with him, ask clarifying questions about his intentions, and see what he has to say after that.

What open communication boils down to is the desire to truly understand each other. It assumes the best of the other person rather than assuming they're selfish or have hurtful intentions—and this can go a long way in any relationship! When are you more likely to have a reasonable discussion with someone—when you're feeling defensive and want to prove you're right, or when you know they believe you have good intentions and will listen to what you say?

In your own relationship, talk about how it would be beneficial for both you and your significant other to communicate in this way. You might communicate *better* if one of you asks clarifying questions and is open and honest about your thoughts, but you'll communicate *best* if both of you are on board.

PRAYER

Ask God to give you the courage to express your thoughts and concerns openly and honestly.

Ask God to always help you give your significant other the benefit of the doubt.

If you know that a difficult conversation is coming up, cover it in prayer and ask God to help you both be reasonable, open, and honest about how you're feeling about the topic.

Leaving and Cleaving

Therefore a man shall leave his father and mother and hold fast to his wife, and they shall become one flesh.

—

Genesis 2:24

The act of "leaving and cleaving" means letting go of other family ties and clinging to your spouse for support, protection, commitment, and anything else you would expect from a marriage relationship. For example, for the most part, you and your future spouse should probably expect to support each other financially (with the exception of special circumstances where help from family might be needed). Or perhaps you're having a problem at work; the first person you go to about it shouldn't be your mother but, rather, your spouse.

You might think of leaving and cleaving as a tenet prescribed only to married couples, not dating or engaged couples. Technically, that's accurate. Before marriage, a couple can and should rely on each other only to a certain extent. Without the covenant of marriage, you don't have the solemn oath before God that you and your partner will support each other and stay committed to each other the way a married couple should. Still, it's important to understand that after you say your marriage vows, the process of leaving and cleaving won't instantly begin as if someone had flipped a switch. Before marriage, as your relationship grows and matures, and as you and your significant other grow and mature as individuals, the concept of leaving and cleaving will become more and more real in your relationship.

As you grow as a couple, you'll have many opportunities to develop and "flex" your independence as a couple. If you don't already attend church together, where will you decide to attend and serve once you're married? Whether or not your families live close by or far apart, will you choose to live close to one of them (and if so, which one?), or will you decide to move to a completely different area?

While you're dating, you and your partner will still have certain boundaries in place, and your ties to your families will be stronger than your ties to each other. As your relationship progresses, though, you can expect your ties to your families to loosen and your ties to each other to strengthen. You'll begin making important decisions together. And while wise input from family members may never totally disappear, you and your significant other will become better and better about making decisions for yourselves, apart from your families.

There may even come a day when your families do not agree with your decisions. A few years ago, Josh and I were fundraising for a short-term mission trip with our church to a country in which outwardly preaching the Gospel was illegal. Our family members advised us not to go, and a few refused to support us. Josh and I respectfully considered their concerns and prayed over the matter, and God used that opportunity to confirm to us that it was still okay to go, even without overwhelming support from our families. So we went in good faith, performed the ministry we had prepared, and returned home safely to our son. Even if our trip had not gone so well, Josh and I believe that because we took the decision to God as a married couple, rather than only heeding the words of our families, we were ultimately where God needed us to be, no matter what.

In your own relationship, examine the areas where you and your significant other cleave to each other and where you still cleave to your families. Are there areas where you seek out the support of your families when you should be seeking it from each other? Are there areas where you're prematurely cleaving to each other when it may still be wise to take the counsel of your families? Over the course of your relationship and into your future marriage, which of those areas do you think will have to change?

PRAYER

Ask God to give you and your significant other the wisdom to know when to cleave to your families and when to cleave to each other.

If and when there comes a time to make a decision as a couple other than what your families would advise, do your best to cover it in prayer and know how to communicate with your family respectfully.

Ask that God, over the course of your relationship, strengthen your independence and your ability to make decisions together.

Prioritize Your Time (Together)

The plans of the diligent lead surely to abundance, but everyone who is hasty comes only to poverty.

—

Proverbs 21:5

The beginning of a relationship is often the most thrilling time. When a relationship is new, many of your thoughts drift toward the person you're dating, and you put a lot of effort into planning ways to spend your time together. Dates during this time will likely be more adventurous, more frequent, and, let's admit it, more exciting.

Over time, as you feel more secure in your relationship and it becomes more enduring and stable, you and your significant other will begin to settle into a routine. Sure, there will still be dates and new adventures here and there, but your relationship will begin to fade from being exciting and new, evolving into something that looks more like simply doing life together. Your significant other might come over to do laundry. You might try to grab lunch together on your break from work. Although dinner dates are fun, doing them all the time usually doesn't make sense financially, so the two of you will probably start cooking meals and watching a movie together instead of going out to a restaurant and movie theater.

As it becomes more normal to simply live life with your significant other, and you realize they're probably not going anywhere anytime soon, the amount of time you spend together will become less of a concern. This might sound like a bad thing, but it's really not! Good relationships have a strong sense of security and reliability, and that's great to have, especially if you and your significant other end up getting married someday. But as the two of you settle into a relationship, the risk that you'll become "ships passing in the night" becomes greater. Life is often going to demand a lot from you—that's just a fact. If you notice that the time you spend with your significant other becomes less and less as life gets busier and busier, it's a safe bet that it won't get any easier the longer you're together. I know of many married couples who, as their children start to leave the nest, have to get to know each other all over again, because for years their relationship functioned more as a collaborative partnership than as a loving and intimate marriage.

Instead of allowing routine to do this to your relationship, you can actually take advantage of it. Like the Little River Band sings, you'll have to "take time to make time." Whether you and your significant other are in school, working, raising kids, or in any other time of life, prioritize making time for each other and build it into your routine.

Make sure that your time together is real quality time. Every single day, make sure you have at least one good conversation. I know it doesn't sound like much, but later on in your relationship, that one good conversation per day can make all the difference. Of course, you'll probably talk more than that during the day, but a lot of that talk will be along the lines of, "Could you grab milk on your way home?" or "I had to have a talk with our child about his attitude today."

On top of this, try to have one extended period of time together, just the two of you, per week. It might be a dedicated date night, or it might just be doing errands together—whatever allows you to be together for a longer period of time and have more than one of those quality conversations. Of course, different stages of life might interrupt these weekly dates, but do your best to come back to this type of routine when you can.

In the appendix (page 158), you'll find 12 date ideas, one for each month of the year. If you're ever short on ideas, try incorporating them into your regular date nights.

PRAYER

When life gets too busy and you feel like you're rushing through your day, ask God to help you see what activities and responsibilities you can cut down on in order to create more opportunities for quality time with your significant other.

Ask God to bless your communication so you and your significant other can have those quality conversations often and are able to reconnect each and every day.

Let Your Yes Be Yes and Your No Be No

"But I say to you, Do not take an oath at all, either by heaven, for it is the throne of God, or by the earth, for it is his footstool. . . . Let what you say be simply 'Yes' or 'No'; anything more than this comes from evil."
—
Matthew 5:34–35, 37

Have you ever told someone you'd do something but secretly hoped they would end up just forgetting about it? Josh and I have done this many times. Josh may say, "Chelsea, I'd like it if you would help me be more accountable for my food choices." I say, "Sure, no problem," but what will I do the next time *I* have a craving for ice cream? I could bring some home and sit in a dark corner of the garage, eating it out of sight. Or maybe I could eat it in front of him and just tell him he can't have any? Neither of those options seems very sustainable or supportive. If I'm going to be the best support possible for him and hold him accountable in any meaningful way, I probably need to apply the same rules to my own life. Maybe I decide I don't want to or can't do that—but in that case, I should say no up front, not say yes and then go back on it.

Here's another example. While Josh has always been very loyal and great at scheduling quality time with me, he used to lose track of time when he was out with friends. He may have told me he'd be done by nine, but if plans changed in the moment or if he lost track of time, it didn't seem like a big deal to him to stay a few hours later than planned without letting me know. I had to communicate with him that I didn't mind if he wanted to spend more time with his friends, but it was frustrating to wait around for him because of what he'd told me earlier. These days, Josh and I are both better at being honest with ourselves and with each other about when we'll be able to follow through on our word.

In many areas of your relationship, you may be struggling to "let your yes be yes and your no be no," especially in the everyday things. It's easy not to worry too much about your commitment to help your partner eat consistently healthy or stay on budget. I mean, it's not like you're being dishonest or *really* hurting them, so they'll probably forgive you, right? The thing is, the more often our yeses become maybes and our nos become probably nots, the more our words begin to lose their meaning. This is where we often resort to saying, "I promise!" or "I really mean it this time!" (implying you don't mean it at other times).

In your relationship, there will probably be times when you're asked to do certain things or to stop doing certain things. When those times come, take the request seriously. If it's something you can commit to, then do your best to agree and follow through on your commitment. If, on the other hand, you're really not sure your yes would be yes, then be transparent and talk with them about it. If it's really not something you can commit to doing, be sure they understand that, so they don't feel as though you went back on your word later on. If a compromise is possible, do your best to find one that you'll both be able to follow through on.

Practicing transparency can be hard at first, especially if you tend to want to be people-pleasing. It's much easier to say yes to someone at first and then give an excuse later than it is to say, "I'm sorry, no" and risk disappointing them in the moment (even though, later on, they'll probably only be *more* disappointed by a false yes than by a true no). In your relationship, try to be honest about your ability to follow through. That's not to say that you shouldn't try new things for fear of failing—just make sure that what you do commit to is realistic for you.

PRAYER

Ask that God would help you have a clear understanding of your strengths and weaknesses and your ability to take on new commitments.

When telling someone yes and making a new commitment, ask God to help you follow through to the best of your ability.

Thank God for always following through in His promises to us.

Joyfulness in Christ

Count it all joy, my brothers, when you meet trials of various kinds, for you know that the testing of your faith produces steadfastness. And let steadfastness have its full effect, that you may be perfect and complete, lacking in nothing.

—

James 1:2–4

As I write this week's devotion, I reflect on the memorial service we held for Josh's grandfather. During the service, many people shared memories of Grandpa's contagious and undying joy. Even as he neared the end of his life, he looked toward the future with joy, knowing that he would soon be face-to-face with the reason for his joy.

The remarkable thing about the joy that Grandpa had was that, no matter the circumstances, his demeanor remained consistently the same. How often do we allow ourselves to be brought down by the circumstances we face? We give ourselves excuses for being in a bad mood or having a poor attitude when we're stressed (or even just hungry). When someone upsets us, we quickly allow ourselves to believe that they are unworthy of kindness and patience.

Of course, Jesus warns us that even (or *especially*) those who believe and hope in Him will have trials in this world: "I have said these things to you, that in me you may have peace. In the world you will have tribulation. But take heart; I have overcome the world" (John

16:33). As you can see in this week's verse, the book of James gives us advice on how to remain joyful through these trials. What is the reason it gives for remaining joyful, even through difficult circumstances? Being steadfast and lacking nothing.

How often do we, as Christians, experience highs and lows, wavering on where we believe we stand with regard to God? One day, we may feel completely in sync with God's will, and the next we may feel distant from God and struggle to feel His presence in our lives. While every Christian goes through those times, our faith in Christ's promises should never falter. We know that God is always the same and that our status with Him remains the same after we're saved, and we can use that steadfastness to find peace in any and every circumstance.

Even on what seem like terrible days, when we remember how much we have been forgiven and how loving Christ is toward us, it can turn a bad attitude into gratitude for Christ's love and forgiveness. Even if we and the people in our lives are inconsistent and let each other down, we can find joy in the fact that God is always consistent and true to His promises. If our life doesn't look how we hoped it would look by now, we can rejoice in the fact that we have hope in a future with Christ—a future that far outweighs any future we can make for ourselves here on earth.

Together with your significant other, practice finding comfort in Christ through situations both easy and difficult. Speak joy into each other's lives when you're going through difficult times, and remind each other that Christ is the only true giver of joy. Make it your goal that others become more joyful as a result of being around you. Turn the conversation toward thankfulness and hopefulness rather than negativity and complaints. If you're known for your joy, you will be making Christ known, to each other and to others.

PRAYER

Ask that God would fill your hearts and minds with joy and thankfulness through every circumstance.

Ask that God would show you examples of joy through trials when reading His Word.

Ask that God would help you encourage others to be joyful, thankful, and steadfast in their relationship with Him.

Love and Money

And he said to them, "Take care, and be on your guard against all covetousness, for one's life does not consist in the abundance of his possessions."

—

Luke 12:15

How important is money to you and your significant other? In high school, I remember my psychology teacher once saying, "When you're young, stability and wealth don't matter that much." In terms of romantic relationships, that means that when you're young, you might believe that you and your significant other can live on love, and you don't care if you have to eat hot dogs for dinner every night, as long as you're with each other. When you get older, however, that starts to change.

Every couple has different levels of ambition, of course, but when Josh and I were young and in love, we mostly just cared about being together. Fast-forward to now, and we have a few more things on our minds. We have two kids to care for, debt to pay off, and rent to make, not to mention we're saving up for a house of our own. It seems as though the more money we have, the more money leaves and goes to other places. And even though we're in one of the most financially stable periods we've ever been in, our life is far from being completely free of stress.

So how can we tell if we have a healthy, godly view of money? We need to remember that money does not satisfy all needs, and it does not create long-lasting joy. Check your bank statements—accounting and budgeting isn't the most exciting way to spend time, but taking a look at where your money goes on a monthly basis can be a great indicator of your priorities. If a large portion of your budget is spent on movies or electronics, you may struggle with putting too much value on entertainment and things that pass the time. If your budget goes toward clothes and accessories, you might be grappling with materialistic tendencies. It's important to note that just because you buy new curtains for your home or go see a movie with your friends, that doesn't necessarily mean you're overvaluing these things. But looking at what percentage of your income goes where will tell you what you prioritize.

While you and your significant other probably have independent finances at this point in your relationship, it's important to develop habits now that will continue into your married lives. The very first step in making sure that your heart and finances are in the right place is to hold your finances and spending habits with an open hand, letting God lead you forward. If you look at your monthly bank statement and see unhealthy spending patterns, don't cling to them. It will take humility and a willingness to change to alter those habits.

Of course, altering your spending habits is only an outward symptom of what might be an underlying issue of the heart. Is overspending on entertainment a sign that you're unsatisfied with your life right now? Do materialistic tendencies indicate a deeper longing for status or a sense of security? Ultimately, if Christ is at the forefront of your life, your spending habits will be a reflection of that. If that's not the case for us, we know our hearts require some adjusting. This, of course, cannot happen without prayer and intentional time spent with Christ. By spending time with Him and setting aside time every day to align your thoughts with His, you will eventually see your spending habits do the same.

PRAYER

Ask God to reveal to you areas of spending that might be excessive.

Ask God to reveal to you the underlying reasons for why your spending may be excessive in certain areas.

Ask God to help you hold your finances with an open hand and not cling to them if He leads you in a different direction.

Loving Confrontation

"If your brother sins against you, go and tell him his fault, between you and him alone. If he listens to you, you have gained your brother. But if he does not listen, take one or two others along with you, that every charge may be established by the evidence of two or three witnesses. If he refuses to listen to them, tell it to the church."

—

Matthew 18:15–17

This week's devotion is about confrontation between you and your significant other. If you haven't had much confrontation yet, know that it will happen eventually, and you'll have learned a great skill set if you can handle it with grace, forgiveness, and honesty.

That said, even if we do handle confrontation in all the right ways, it doesn't always guarantee the outcome we're looking for. By confronting someone, you're asking for some type of change, but what if the person isn't ready to make that change? What if they don't feel they're able to change, don't see a good reason to change, or simply don't want to change? What do we do then? It's here you'll need to spend extra time in prayer and consideration.

One possibility is that the change you would like to see isn't necessarily something that God would ask. Sure, it might be good and helpful, but it's not biblically *required*. Let's say, for example, your significant other has a habit of leaving their things all over the place.

You might lovingly talk to them about their habit of leaving a mess, let them know how it makes you feel, and ask them to change. Change would be nice, but a godly approach to this particular situation isn't explicitly discussed in the Bible. In this case, you'll have to keep praying, keep communicating with your partner, and hope that with time, you can make headway on the issue.

But another possibility is that you're asking for a change you know without a doubt is discussed in the Bible. For example, you might find that your significant other struggles with a sexual temptation like pornography, or maybe they've been dishonest. In that case, when you confront them, you can use Scripture to remind them of the standard that Christ sets for Christians. Of course, everyone struggles with different sins and we all fall short of Christ's standards, so it's important to follow His example of forgiveness and understanding. That being said, it is okay for Christians to hold other Christians accountable, as in this week's Bible verse, as long as we're also showing grace and doing our best to live by those standards ourselves. So what do you do if your partner digs in their heels on a change that's commanded by the Bible?

In His time on earth, Jesus provided great advice on how to confront fellow Christians well. Step one, as Matthew 18 outlines, is to speak with the person privately. In a best-case scenario, you'd discuss it together openly and support each other as you work on making the change. But if they refuse to listen, take it to a couple of fellow believers whom you trust and have good relationships with, and see if they agree with your assessment of the situation. These people might be among your significant other's friends, mentors, or family members. If you, together with these people, are unable to help your significant other turn away from their sin, the next thing Jesus suggests is taking it to the church. While I don't recommend calling out your significant other's sin in front of the entire church congregation, having a pastor, elder, or other trusted church leader pray and give counsel would be the next step to take. Your significant other will probably feel defensive at first, but the goal is to lovingly show them that the change you're asking for is specifically addressed in Scripture, and that friends, family, and members of the church are also calling for this change.

The hope is that one of these acts of confrontation in love will inspire your partner to work toward cutting out the sin they've been struggling with. Of course, they're not going to magically become perfect immediately after your conversation, but you're not asking for perfection. You're asking to see a heart that desires change and takes actionable steps toward it. If your significant other is unwilling to do that, then you have a hard choice about whether or not to stay in a relationship with someone who clearly refuses to live by God's Word, whether or not they refer to themselves as a Christian.

Situations like this are often messy and have many gray areas. But if we make decisions based on our love for Christ and truly seek to please Him, we will find ourselves in the midst of God's will, even when it's not perfectly clear to us whether to go left or right.

PRAYER

Pray that, if you are confronted by your significant other about sin in your life, God would prepare your heart ahead of time to receive the confrontation with grace and a humble attitude.

Pray that God would always give you a spirit of grace and humility, so that when it comes time to confront a friend or significant other, they can see that you're doing it out of love rather than pridefulness.

Remember to cover any and all confrontation with prayer so you and the person you are confronting both desire an outcome that brings glory to God.

All for God's Glory

So, whether you eat or drink, or whatever you do,
do all to the glory of God.
—

1 Corinthians 10:31

Whether you're a full-time student, working full time or part time, or volunteering, there may come a moment when you stop and think, *Am I really making a difference? Is my job really worth it in the long run?*

Both Josh and I have struggled with this question. Even when I worked as an administrative assistant for our church, I would sometimes question if my job really mattered. And for Josh, working in an IT department and staring at computer screens all day, it often felt like he was missing out on real ministry opportunities and the ability to make a difference in people's lives. Over time, this began to really bother him, and it seemed to have a constant effect on his mood and how he felt about leaving for work every morning. And when one person's mood is unhappy and dissatisfied, it can't help but affect their significant other and the relationship they share.

Noticing this, we began to pray together about his job and his feelings about it. Josh also started to have encouraging conversations with some of the men in our Bible study who also had jobs that weren't directly related to ministry. He began to realize that although the work he was performing didn't *directly* feed the hungry and clothe the poor, he was still doing work that God had called him to. As a husband, he was protecting and providing for his family. As a member of God's church, he was living in community with other Christians. As a light to the world, he was setting an example and preaching the Gospel through his work ethic and conversations with nonbelievers at work.

Do you and your significant other ever get down when you feel as though work (or school or other responsibilities) gets in the way of ministry and "real life"? If you do, remind each other that Christ isn't present only where the needy are being cared for. He is just as present in your office, your commute, and even your morning routine. In each of those settings, you have the ability to experience God's presence as well as make a difference in the lives of others.

Besides, your workplace isn't the only place where you have the ability to minister to people. You and your significant other can use some of the time you have together for ministry opportunities that God calls you to. Grow in community with other Christians by joining a small group Bible study where you can meet and serve others within your own church. And while you might not have as much time to devote purely to ministry and making a difference as you might like, it doesn't mean your life will *always* look that way. Life circumstances frequently end up changing more often than we think they will. Who knows? Six months or a few years from now, you may have more time for ministry than you expected.

That said, it's important to live life in the moment and make the most of the time you have today. We have no guarantees of what life will look like in the future, and getting in the habit of living a Christ-centered life in the moment will ensure that you live your life—your whole life—for Christ, no matter what circumstances you find yourself in.

In Luke 12, Jesus tells a parable about a man who worked hard in the beginning of his life and planned to store his ample earnings in barns so he could live out the rest of his days however he wanted. Little did he know that that night would be his last and he would never get to enjoy what he had been waiting to enjoy his whole life. My point is this: Don't wait until "someday" to get more involved in ministry and serve others for Christ. You and your partner can do so with the time you have now, setting an example for others about how to live their lives in a way that makes the most of their situations for Christ's glory.

PRAYER

Ask God to reveal to you ways in which you can show others His love in your workplace, classroom, or any other place you go.

Ask God to help you be joyful and thankful even if your life circumstances are not what you would wish them to be.

Ask God to show you ministry opportunities that you do have the time for.

Ask God to reveal to you which time commitments in your life are unnecessary and could be replaced with something that feels more meaningful.

Taking Healthy Time Apart

And rising very early in the morning, while it was still dark,
he departed and went out to a desolate place, and there he prayed.
—

Mark 1:35

During the very beginning of our relationship, Josh and I spent all our free time together, and I mean all of it. If we weren't sleeping, using the bathroom, or in class, we were together. And to be honest, it made a lot of our other relationships suffer. I went to college with two of my best friends, and by the end of the school year, my relationship with them wasn't anywhere near where it had been at the beginning.

Josh and I were almost literally inseparable, and while we had a very communicative and close relationship, the amount of time we spent together probably did more harm than good. It put too much pressure on each of us and shut us out somewhat from our friends and other godly influences. When Josh and I struggled with, for example, physical temptation, talking to our friends about it and seeking accountability wasn't as easy as it would have been had we been better about keeping up those other relationships.

If or when you and your significant other get married someday, leaving and cleaving (see week 2, page 4) will be something both of you will have to practice during your early years of marriage. But healthy friendships with people who are not your spouse will still be important even after you're married! This is even truer while you're dating or engaged. No matter where you are in your relationship with your significant other, it can only benefit you to surround yourself with godly friends who want to see you have a thriving relationship with Christ.

Too much time spent with a significant other often means that one or both of you might struggle with insecurities that make it uncomfortable to face life situations without the other close by as a sort of "safe person." When uncomfortable situations come up, like struggles at work, conflict with roommates, or even just not wanting to be alone when eating a meal, it feels better when your "safe person" is there. And although dating a person you can trust, do life with, and confide in is great, when couples start using each other as a shield from the difficult things in life, a sense of codependence, rather than autonomy, can begin to grow.

While I'm not going to tell you that you have to spend at least two nights per week apart from your significant other (though I do suggest it), I do want to ask you to self-evaluate. Sure, you're going to want to spend a lot of time together, and that's fine. But ask yourselves if you're spending excessive amounts of time together instead of with friends, in ministry, or simply being alone with yourself (which we all need from time to time). Ask yourself if you're using your significant other as a kind of security blanket rather than taking difficult situations to God and learning how to face them on your own. Ask yourself if you've been too neglectful of godly friendships and influences in your lives and, if so, how you can divide your time in a way that prioritizes those relationships as well.

In the end, when we bring our struggles to God and remember that our value doesn't change even during what feel like low points, we can go through life with our confidence intact and feel less reliant on having that safe person nearby. If we can remember that God gave us the ability to be intelligent and stand on His strength, dealing with difficult situations independently won't seem nearly as daunting. Of course, this is only possible if we consistently reflect on our relationship with Christ and spend time learning more about who He is and how valuable we are to Him.

PRAYER

Ask God to bring godly friendships into the lives of both you and your significant other.

If you struggle with this, ask God to help you feel confident and comfortable spending short periods of time apart to reflect or even enjoy yourself without your boyfriend or girlfriend having to be with you.

Ask God to remind you of the value you hold in His eyes and that difficult situations or people can't take that away.

The Right Way to Apologize

Therefore, confess your sins to one another and pray for one another, that you may be healed.
—

James 5:16

We can be so quick to try to convince the world that something is anyone's fault but ours, can't we?

I admit I'm an expert when it comes to this. For example, I'm perpetually late, as Josh likes to remind me. In fact, he says that if you added up all the minutes and hours, he's probably spent many days simply *waiting* for me. My dad liked to say that I lived in my own time zone growing up. And every time I'm late, I find some reason that puts it outside my control. Before I had kids, I was late because my alarm didn't go off, I got stuck behind the train, there was traffic, or it was "just hard to get out of the house today" (I love that one). Now that I have kids, I can say I'm late because of them (they're a good excuse for pretty much anything). I almost never just come out and say, "I decided to hit the snooze button too many times," or "I went through my entire closet before deciding on something to wear."

Don't we often do the same thing in our relationships with friends, family, significant others, and even coworkers? Say you forgot to send an important e-mail, or you put off telling your mom that you would be visiting your partner's family instead of hers for Christmas this year. If you're like most of us, your first line of defense is to tell those you let down *why* you let them down. Maybe you hasten to explain that you had a lot of other projects on your mind, or you were afraid to upset your mom. And while explaining yourself isn't necessarily bad, using it as a substitute for an apology is.

When we use excuses in place of apologies, we miss out on opportunities to grow and also to reconcile with the people we let down. Excuses say, "I'm really not responsible for letting you down, and you'll need to make up for it yourself," whereas apologies say, "I messed up, and I know I should have done better. I want to improve from here on out." Apologies, when sincere, imply that we understand our fault and want to do better, both for our sake and for the sake of others.

When we apologize to one another as believers, it allows us to be united with our brothers and sisters in Christ. When we apologize to those who are nonbelievers, it sets an example of humility, conveying that we know we're imperfect and in need of a savior. And when we apologize to our significant others, it helps build trust and love, with each other and with God.

It's also important to point out that the *need* to apologize doesn't always occur at the same time we *feel* like apologizing. You could even be completely unaware that you offended anyone. If and when your significant other addresses with you something you did that hurt or frustrated them, you might feel defensive and want to explain your way out of their accusation. Instead, pause and listen to that voice in your head telling you that you should probably just apologize because your action was likely inconsiderate. Then, perhaps later, after reading Scripture and humbling yourself before God, you'll feel the conviction of your apology.

In Scripture, I often find that God cares about us keeping peace with the people in our lives, not exhausting ourselves trying to figure out who was right. When you get into a disagreement with your significant other, you'll often find that the blame can be shared between the two of you. Even so, make it your personal goal to be the first to apologize, even if your partner isn't convinced they have anything to apologize for. As frustrating as it might feel in the moment, be sure that your apology comes out of sincerity instead of a desire to manipulate your significant other into apologizing as well. You can go on peacefully understanding that you have done what Christ would want you to do in an effort to keep the peace and remain humble in your relationship. From there, you can pray for your significant other that God would work in their heart and reveal to them any fault of theirs.

Any godly relationship that goes below the surface will require humility and apologies from time to time. Having a clear understanding of yourself, your imperfect nature, and your need for a savior will make apologizing quickly much easier and more natural. Do your best to constantly spend time in God's Word and in prayer so that you can daily align your heart with the things of God.

PRAYER

Ask God to give you a spirit of humility so you can quickly recognize when you're at fault.

Ask God to help you be humble enough to be the first to apologize, even when you don't feel like it.

Ask God to help you apologize with no strings attached.

True Christian Community

Two are better than one, because they have a good reward for their toil. For if they fall, one will lift up his fellow. But woe to him who is alone when he falls and has not another to lift him up!
—

Ecclesiastes 4:9–10

The longer you and your significant other date, the more you may become reliant on each other. Previously, when you wanted to go out and grab a bite for dinner, you may have called up a friend, but now, more often than not, you ask your boyfriend or girlfriend to join you. While you used to confide in your friends, you now confide in your fiancé(e). And while maintaining friendships throughout your relationship and even in marriage is healthy, experiencing life with your significant other is a natural part of growing together and will continue into marriage and beyond.

This being the case, I often see couples go in and out of stages of isolation from others. The more a couple is able to depend and rely on each other, the less they feel a need for outside resources. This is especially true for newlyweds, as they're often moving to new places and entering a completely new stage of life, but it's also true for seriously dating and engaged couples as well. You may find that even if you and your boyfriend or girlfriend attend church together (which is great), the relationships you have with the people there don't go much beyond smiling and saying hi on your way out the door.

If this sounds like you, even if you feel like it more or less at different times, you're not alone. Josh and I are both introverted types and didn't put much effort into building relationships at our church for the first several years we attended. But after we were married for a couple of years, we began to feel a longing for Christian relationships outside of each other. Not that there was anything significantly wrong with our marriage, but we knew we could only build each other up so much, and there came a point when we needed true Christian community.

We decided to join a small group Bible study and begin serving in ways that we felt we could maintain even with our work schedules and our first baby. The first several weeks of going to Bible study felt forced, and to be honest, somewhat awkward. To gather in a room with complete strangers and be open and vulnerable felt unnatural. But over time, as we served together, spent time together, and did more things together with our small group, we began to wonder how we ever got along without them.

Because we started building relationships with other godly couples in our church, we were consistently being prayed for, we had people rooting for not only our marriage but also our relationship with Christ, and we had wise friends to seek out when hard times came. These were the type of friends who told us what we *needed* to hear instead of what we *wanted* to hear. Ultimately, they wanted both Josh and me to have a great relationship with Christ. And we wanted the same for them, so we would pray and counsel them in the same way, the best way we could—with God's help. As we did, our relationship with God (and even with each other) became less about ourselves and more about the body of Christ. Overall, we prayed more, served more, and ultimately cared more for people outside our relationship. God taught us that loving imperfect people, especially those different from us, is an integral part of being part of His church.

If you find that you and your significant other are living in relative isolation (with each other), I encourage you to reach out and find a

Christian community that will pray for you, build you up, and be honest with you when you need to hear honest words. I think a great way to do this is by joining a small group Bible study, but that isn't the only way to build Christian relationships. You can also grow your community by serving, being more intentional when attending church services, or simply taking the initiative to reach out to new or old friends. God never said that life, especially a Christian one, would be easy, but He also never intended for Christians to go it alone.

PRAYER

Ask that God would show you ways you can reach out and start building a community of like-minded believers.

Ask God to give you the strength and confidence to take initiative when building relationships.

Ask that God would bring godly relationships into your and your significant other's lives.

Ask God to use you to build up other Christians and be the community for others who may be feeling isolated.

Challenge Each Other

And we urge you, brothers, admonish the idle, encourage the faithhearted, help the weak, be patient with them all.

—

1 Thessalonians 5:14

If I could have a conversation with myself but eight years younger, the two selves would probably barely even recognize each other. My eight-years-ago self had extreme insecurities, an unhealthy fear of authority, different aims in life, no health or fitness goals even on the radar, and let's just say my sense of style was ... eclectic. Josh, too, was a very different person when we met eight years ago. Today, we are parents, we have relatively clear career goals, health and fitness is a major part of our lives, and insecurities and authority figures aren't things we worry about anymore.

So what changed? Did we simply grow up and mature?

Well, yes, but it's not that simple. A big part of our growth and maturity came from us challenging each other. Josh's family was very into health and fitness, so you can imagine where my relatively new passion for that comes from. Josh was and continues to be very good at being direct and honest with people, so it was only a matter of time before I was forced to overcome my fear of confrontation. In the same way, Josh, who was not always the best at empathizing with others, over time became very empathetic and compassionate with those he met, because those qualities are important to me.

During the course of our dating relationship and up to the present, Josh and I have always challenged each other to grow in new ways. Much of this is the result of assuming the best of each other. It's very difficult to encourage someone to grow if they feel judged. If I had acted like Josh was a horrible, mean person because he was not always empathetic, asking him to grow would have felt like an ultimatum, command, or judgment rather than a grace-filled call for change. In the same way, if I had felt like Josh wouldn't love me unless I pursued health and fitness, I would have done it begrudgingly and out of fear, if at all.

Challenging each other can be a great way for both you and your significant other to grow together in your relationship. You can develop new hobbies and characteristics that are similar to each other's and, as a result, become more unified and in sync. However, asking for change must always be done with love and respect. If the person who is being asked to change has any fear of judgment or ultimatums, we can hardly expect the change to be genuine or done out of love.

We see a parallel of this in Christ's relationship to the church. When Christ gave Himself up for the church, He did so in order to make her holy. In other words, with love and grace and no condition except belief, He calls her to change for the better: "Husbands, love your wives, as Christ loved the church and gave himself up for her, that he might sanctify her . . . that she might be holy and without blemish" (Ephesians 5:25–27).

This concept can be applied to many aspects of your relationship, whether you're asking your significant other to communicate better, take on more responsibility, or simply pursue a goal they've been talking about for a while. When challenging your significant other, let them know that you love them whether or not they accept and pursue the challenge, that you're here to encourage them, and that you believe they can live up to the challenge. Then do your best to be an example to them and continue to support them. Be sure to communicate the goals you're working toward as well. Be open with your partner about areas where you want to grow and challenge yourself, and ask them to lovingly hold you accountable in those areas.

PRAYER

Ask God to allow both you and your significant other to meet the goals and challenges you set for yourselves.

Ask God to help you align your goals with His will, so you and your significant other can also be in sync with them.

Ask God to help you support your significant other in reaching their goals and rising to new challenges.

Ask that God would allow you to accept challenges from your significant other with a spirit of humility, understanding that there's always room to grow.

Finding Unity in Conflict

Walk worthy of the calling you have received, with all humility and gentleness, with patience, accepting one another in love, diligently keeping the unity of the Spirit with the peace that binds us. There is one body and one Spirit . . . one Lord, one faith, one baptism, one God and Father of all, who is above all and through all and in all.

—

Ephesians 4:1–6 (HCSB)

How do you and your significant other fight?

When I was young, I used to think that the best couples never fought. Sure, they disagreed—no couple can agree on everything for 20 or 30 or 50-plus years—but when they disagreed, I assumed they did it gracefully and trusted each other to know what was best, and that the one who conceded usually trusted the other to be right.

Fast-forward a few years, and Josh and I didn't even have to walk down the aisle before I realized just how rare that kind of relationship was. Couples fight. The best ones, the worst ones, almost every one. But it's the *way* couples fight that's really important.

Before Josh and I got married, we had a few big fights. After we got married, we had a lot of big fights. Even if you and your future spouse check off all the same things on a long list of fundamental beliefs, you'd probably both be surprised at how many things you disagree on once you begin a life together. Things like whether or not it's acceptable to do the dishes three times in a row without your significant other offering to help. Or how accepting one of you is about their family's weirdness (or even sinfulness). Or where you each draw your respective lines about what's okay to joke about or watch on TV.

These differences could, and very well may, start a fight from time to time—and that's fine, as long as you remember your end goal. Keeping your end goal in mind may not prevent you from disagreeing, but it will completely change the *way* you disagree or even fight.

What is that goal? According to Paul in this week's Bible verse, it's this: When living among other Christians, even the ones we find annoying, we must be "diligently keeping the unity of the Spirit with the peace that binds us" (Ephesians 4:3 HCSB). If you do this, you'll begin to see disagreements as a way to work things out and *reconcile*, rather than as a way to heatedly prove your point, say what you've been secretly thinking for weeks, or finally make the other person a little more like you and less like themselves. When your goal is to be unified in Christ (so you can live for Him more effectively), it's easier to remember to be slow to anger, to understand the person with whom you have a disagreement, and to seek a solution that works for both of you *and* is pleasing to God.

If you continue reading Ephesians 4, you'll see that Paul lists several different functions and roles within the body of Christ—evangelists, prophets, apostles, teachers, and so on. Christ knew (and revealed to Paul) that individual Christians would be vastly different from one another in both their spiritual gifts and their sinful (or just annoying) tendencies.

This is why Paul calls us to "walk worthy of the calling" (Ephesians 4:1 HCSB). Although each Christian is called to a new life in Christ (for which other Christians can hold them accountable), forgiving and being forbearing with one another is a very regular part of that. We do this as we follow the example of Christ, the one who unified us all in Himself. The greatest part about this is that while we forgive each other *for* Christ, we also are able to do this only *through* Christ. Living in peace with other Christians, starting with your significant other, is essential for working together for Christ's glory, as well as being a picture of His love to the world.

Work and Worry

"Peace I leave with you; my peace I give to you. Not as the world gives do I give to you. Let not your hearts be troubled, neither let them be afraid."
—

John 14:27

There was a time in my life when I was genuinely unstressed. Although life wasn't perfect, I had no big worries or concerns about the immediate or distant future. At the time, I was a stay-at-home mom, blogging from home, and I couldn't imagine a situation in which I'd want to be doing anything else.

Fast-forward a few months, and Josh and I found ourselves in somewhat of a financial strain. After weeks of talks, Josh and I finally decided it would be best for the whole family if I sought full-time employment. At first, I was excited at the chance to test some new skills I had learned through my blogging career, but after the excitement of landing a new job wore off and the expectations of me grew and grew, so did my stress level. I remember thinking that as long as I could wake up early, go to bed late, and work my hardest throughout the day, we would be okay. But no matter how much work I got done during a day and no matter how many times I succeeded or failed, I never seemed to evade worry.

During that time, I found myself lacking in receiving the Word and spending quality time in prayer. My stress and worry caused me to put most things, including my relationship with God, on the back burner while I did my best to work hard and provide what my family needed. What I had forgotten was that even if my family and I had all the financial stability in the world, we would still be completely lost without an intimate relationship with Jesus. The example I was setting for them was one of self-sustainability rather than reliance on Christ.

When I began to have quiet moments with Christ on a daily basis, it didn't necessarily mean that my workload changed or that I could stop getting up early and going to bed late, but it did change my perspective of the work I was doing and how I felt throughout it. I could see my work from an eternal point of view, one that reminded me that the work is temporary, our lives are temporary, but Christ and heaven are eternal.

I've always loved a quote commonly attributed to Martin Luther. When asked what his plans for the next day were, he said, "Work, work, from early until late. In fact, I have so much to do that I shall spend the first three hours in prayer." It's my belief that Martin Luther truly understood the responsibility he had to convey God's Word accurately. And this didn't only happen through his writing; it happened largely through his speech and actions as well. Spending so much time in prayer wasn't just more important than his everyday duties; it had the happy side effect of making those duties easier for him to handle.

No matter what jobs or responsibilities we have, as Christians our ultimate goal—a goal that transcends all other work and responsibilities—is to overflow with Christ's love and truth. We can only do that when we're already filled up with God's Word, which means it's extremely important to regularly spend time reading the Bible, learning from other godly people, and spending time in community with others in the church.

This is something you and your significant other can help each other with. When one of you is under a lot of stress, you can remind each other of God's centrality and primacy in your lives and spend some of your time together talking and praying about the issue. Yes, this is something that takes time out of your day, but it's also something you'll take with you into your work and other responsibilities, as well as your relationships. And that's what will make all the difference when those who are nonbelievers look at you and see that although you could be bogged down by stress and worry, you are overflowing with truth and love. As Jesus said, "By this all people will know that you are my disciples, if you have love for one another" (John 13:35).

PRAYER

Thank God for leaving us His spirit and providing us a way to always be in tune with Him.

Ask God to help you set aside time each day for reading His Word and bringing your concerns to Him in prayer.

If you're feeling stressed and bogged down, ask God to encourage you, uplift your spirit, and give you a sense of peace throughout your work and other responsibilities.

Family Matters

"Honor your father and your mother, that your days may be long in the land that the LORD your God is giving you."
—

Exodus 20:12

If you and your significant other have been dating for a while, you've probably had at least a few talks about your respective families. Have you had a chance to meet each other's family yet? If so, what was your initial impression, and how did you all get along?

In week 2 (page 4), we discussed "leaving and cleaving," and how important it is to leave the family you grew up with behind and establish yourself as an individual, creating a new family with your future spouse. I believe that happens in earnest upon getting married, but some parts of the process may begin before marriage. And as much as you and your future spouse may want to cleave to each other once you're married, you're almost guaranteed to interact with each other's families with varying degrees of frequency. You may live across the country from your family, but you'll still probably talk on the phone, chat via the Internet, and visit each other now and then.

As much as any dating or married couple is its own individual unit, people do come with families. And one day, if you and your significant other decide to tie the knot, you'll become part of each other's larger families as well. While a close family can be a wonderful support system, not everyone lucks out with a family that's easy to get along with, cheers them on, and supports their independence. Every family situation is different. You or your significant other may have family members who are overbearing or insensitive, or who don't have a great relationship with Christ.

Whatever your situation, remember that while your partner is their own person, it's important to respect the family they come from. You'll likely have times where the two of you disagree with one of your families on one point or another, and while you may decide to stand your ground, learning how to respond with grace and tact will go a long way in your relationships with your respective families and with each other.

Setting clear boundaries and expectations with your significant other and their family will help everyone avoid frustration and hurt feelings in the future. For example, if both families expect you to visit every Christmas, but you can only visit one family per year, do your best to explain the conundrum to each family and ask them to compromise, perhaps by switching off between them every year. If they're determined not to listen, you might have to set a firm boundary with a simple statement such as, "I'm sorry, but we just won't be able to make it this year." But often, I find that explaining or even overexplaining a situation is a better choice. Even if an explanation isn't strictly necessary, it may help soothe tensions and repair feelings in the long run.

There are often times, for example, when my family (who live in New Jersey) ask Josh and me (who live in Washington State) to come visit them with the kids. When that doesn't work for us, I explain in detail why the timing isn't right or why it wouldn't be beneficial for us to travel, and how my decision has nothing to do with not loving them or not wanting to see them. Even though some disappointment is inevitable, everyone leaves the conversation with their feelings intact.

Of course, any struggles you and your significant other have with your families may not be about travel or the amount of time you spend with them. It could be about religious beliefs, values, or even personalities in general. Whatever the case, remember week 13's lesson of unity (page 37), and how Paul encourages believers "to walk in a manner worthy of the calling to which you have been called, with all humility and gentleness, with patience, bearing with one another in love, eager

to maintain the unity of the Spirit in the bond of peace"
(Ephesians 4:1–3).

Think of your interactions with each other's families as opportunities to show Christ's love and mercy. Sure, they may be aggravating at times, but Christ didn't die only for the people you find agreeable and nonfrustrating. He died for you, your significant other, and all of your family members, and He desires for each and every one of you to know Him personally.

PRAYER

Pray that Christ would give you the ability to show extra love and grace to each of your family members.

Pray that you would be slow to speak, slow to anger, and quick to listen.

Pray that you would use your opportunities wisely to be a picture of God's grace to each member of your family.

Acknowledge Your Insecurities

And I am sure of this, that he who began a good work in you will bring it to completion at the day of Jesus Christ.
—

Philippians 1:6

When Josh and I entered into a relationship, I thought he was pretty much perfect. (Sure, there were a few flaws, but everyone has their quirks.) One of the reasons I looked up to Josh so much was the fact that he always seemed to be so confident. Talking to people came easily to him, he could always make his friends laugh, and he was never afraid to ask questions.

I, on the other hand, was always one of the last to speak whenever we were with a group. I've always enjoyed listening over talking, but what went much deeper than that was my fear of sounding silly. Josh didn't know when we started dating that I struggled with deep insecurities and always worried about how people perceived me, which made me act unnatural or awkward in certain situations. He later revealed that he'd noticed this behavior but didn't realize where it was coming from.

Likewise, I didn't realize Josh had some insecurities of his own. When I first met him at the beginning of his college career, his major was undecided. While we dated and even in the beginning of our marriage, he switched his major a few times and even began and dropped out of a couple of technical studies. Little did I know that this was something he was extremely insecure about and hated talking about. There were times when I'd ask him, "What's your dream job? What are you passionate about?" He would get red in the face, shake his head, say, "I don't know," and change the subject. At the time, it was a relatively major setback, because Josh and I were always able to talk about anything . . . except this.

The thing is, as much as Josh and I each didn't want the other to see our embarrassing insecurities, the closer we got to each other, the more noticeable those insecurities became. From the moment we started dating, it was only a matter of time before these issues came out in the open. And once they did, we could have tried to sweep them under the rug (that probably would have felt better in the moment!), but neither Josh nor I wanted a relationship like that. We had to just deal with them.

So, when Josh noticed some of my awkward behavior, he would ask me about it. I wasn't fully aware of the reasons *why* I was acting that way at the time, and his questions made me start to think about it. We talked about it. Josh listened. And eventually, after enough talking about it and after understanding how accepted I was by Josh and by our Savior, I began to grow and, piece by piece, leave some of my insecurities behind. A similar transformation happened with Josh. I asked him why he seemed to get frustrated and embarrassed when I asked him about his career goals. Eventually, he was able to reply that not being as career-driven as many others he knew was a big insecurity for him.

For each of us, it wasn't enough to simply know that our significant other accepted us. Our insecurities went deeper than just our relationship with each other; they also had to do with our relationships with Christ and how secure we felt in Him. If I had been strongly convinced from the start that all that mattered was that Jesus had forgiven me and accepted me, then I would never have spent so much time worrying about what others thought about me. The same goes for Josh. If his security had come from the fact that he is a co-heir with Christ, the fact that he is not as career-minded as some of his peers would not have made him feel like less of a man.

While I am an advocate of "guarding your heart" during dating relationships (see week 28, page 82), I don't recommend revealing a big insecurity you've been hiding from your future husband or wife only *after* you've married. The truth is that there will be times when you and the person you're dating discover insecurities in each other. When you do, be ready to point each other to Christ's love, mercy, and forgiveness. Remind each other that if you're a believer, you're fully accepted by Christ, even as a work in progress.

If you and your significant other have God at the forefront of your relationship and both desire to see the other have a strong, secure relationship with Him, don't be afraid to be open with each other.

PRAYER

Pray for each other in the areas of your insecurities. Praise each other when you show signs of growth or do something outside your comfort zone.

Thank God for making you unique and giving you strengths and weaknesses that allow you to call on God's strengths to supplement your weaknesses.

The Reason for Forgiveness

"And whenever you stand praying, forgive, if you have anything against anyone, so that your Father also who is in heaven may forgive you your trespasses."
—

Mark 11:25

After about a year or so of dating, Josh and I had gotten to know each other pretty well. Although we'd been together for a while, we were experiencing a rough patch in our relationship. One night, after getting dinner together, Josh said something that deeply hurt my feelings. I can't tell you exactly what it was because at this point I don't remember the specific words, but I do remember the feelings: I felt wounded, frustrated, and lonely, because the person I loved the most had done something hurtful.

Josh took a quiet moment to gather his thoughts. Then he came to me and apologized. I was still so mad that I just shook my head and tightened my lips. I didn't feel like forgiving him at all. It wasn't the first time he had said something along the same lines, then apologized for doing it. I was done forgiving it. How would he ever learn if I kept forgiving him?

At that same moment, it felt as though God sent a direct message to my brain: "But I forgave you..."

I immediately started to cry. My unwillingness to forgive Josh had broken my heart because I knew how much I had been forgiven. It's true, Josh had been insensitive with his words. But if Christ is willing to forgive me, an imperfect person prone to sin, how much more should I be willing to forgive another imperfect person?

Growing up, I heard sermons from pastors about how we should forgive because it frees us and helps us let go of bitterness, as if to say we should forgive because it will ultimately make us happier people. The thing is, God doesn't ask believers to forgive so that we'll lead happier lives (even though that is often a side benefit). God commands us to forgive one another because we have been forgiven. God is so serious about His children forgiving others that He says, "For if you forgive others their trespasses, your heavenly Father will also forgive you, but if you do not forgive others their trespasses, neither will your Father forgive your trespasses" (Matthew 6:14–15).

Think about that for a second. That verse is actually in the Bible. God might *not* forgive you—that is, if you refuse to show that same forgiveness to others. How thankful can we really be for God's forgiveness if we withhold forgiveness from others? Are we truly finding our joy solely in Christ if we're unable to forgive the people who let us down?

Think of Luke 7:41–43, in which Jesus shares a parable: "'A certain moneylender had two debtors. One owed five hundred denarii, and the other fifty. When they could not pay, he cancelled the debt of both. Now which of them will love him more?' Simon answered, 'The one, I suppose, for whom he cancelled the larger debt.' And he said to him, 'You have judged rightly.'" The reason Jesus told this story in the first place is because he was at the home of a Pharisee. While he was there, a woman described as a sinner came and anointed Jesus's feet with an entire jar of perfume. When the Pharisee was offended that Jesus was letting a sinful woman touch Him, Jesus answered him with the parable above. He finishes the lesson by saying, "Therefore I tell you, her sins, which are many, are forgiven—for she loved much. But he who is forgiven little, loves little" (Luke 7:47).

How often do we hear the phrase "forgive and forget"? It's good advice to a large extent, but I believe that God doesn't want us to forget our own sins completely. I believe He wants us to have a healthy remembrance of our past guilt so we can be that much more grateful for the fact that we have been forgiven and now live in freedom. Not that we need to go about our lives feeling guilt and shame—Christ wants us to find joy in Him! But how can we find joy in Christ if we don't remember how much He did for us? Remembering our sins makes us live in awe of the One who took our place on the cross. It makes us willing to joyfully forgive those who sin against us and need our forgiveness. It helps us point those people to Christ and His forgiveness that covers all sin.

By joyfully forgiving others, especially our significant others, we're remembering that Christ forgives us when we're undeserving. We are making the most of an opportunity to make Christ great in our lives and show Him off to the world.

PRAYER

Ask that God would help you and your significant other rejoice in how much you've been forgiven and live thankful for His forgiveness.

Ask God to help you forgive others even when they let you down or hurt you, remembering how much you have been forgiven.

Ask God to help you use those moments to point both believers and nonbelievers back to the God who forgives.

Meeting Each Other Where You Are

To the weak I became weak, that I might win the weak. I have become all things to all people, that by all means I might save some. I do it all for the sake of the gospel, that I may share with them in its blessings.
—

1 Corinthians 9:22–23

When you make the decision to share your life with someone, I mean *really* share your life with someone, you're bound to get to know all their personality quirks and how those quirks do or don't match your own. For example, your significant other might absolutely hate crowds, which could be a problem if, to you, Disneyland really is the happiest place on earth. It could be something as small as the fact that they like peanut butter *everything* and you're just not a fan. Or it could be that, for whatever reason, they're extremely insecure about something, whether it be a body part, something from their past, or their education or career. The point is, the more time you spend with your significant other (or anyone, for that matter), the more quirks you'll discover about each other.

When Josh and I first started dating, he had no idea how insecure a person he had just started a relationship with. Every so often, he felt he needed to discuss something with me. It might have been about how I was handling my relationship with my roommates, my eating and fitness habits (which were not where I felt they needed to be at the time), or the fact that I was putting off my homework. In my mind, he was telling me how he didn't like me, and to my insecure self, it always felt like an ultimatum: "Fix this thing that's wrong with you, or I'll be unhappy and leave." Of course, that's not what Josh meant at all. He comes from a family that always talked plainly about each other's idiosyncrasies and shortcomings, while my family usually didn't. So when he and I got together and he felt like he needed to talk to me about something, my thought was, *Wow, if he's bringing this up to me it must really be bothering him. He must be so unhappy with me.* But that wasn't the case at all!

And once he discovered why I became so upset or defensive every time he confronted me with an issue, big or small, he figured out that, because of my thought process, he needed to put my mind at ease if he was going to bring something up. He had to remind me that, yes, he still cared about me, and even if he thought I could use some change in one area of my life, that didn't mean he was disappointed in me as a person. Josh changed his approach, reassured me, and eventually I grew out of that quirk and was able to take constructive criticism much better. But it wasn't without a lot of grace and patience and extra love from Josh.

So what does this mean for you? It means that, when certain quirks come up in your own relationship (if you haven't noticed them yet, trust me—you will), do not try to quickly iron out the wrinkles in your significant other. Instead, remember that when you come together in a relationship, you're bringing together two very different people. Sure, dating relationships aren't necessarily permanent, and the person you're dating may have some habits or traits you decide would be better to live without. (If Josh was criticizing me cruelly or trying to prove he was superior to me, that probably would have been a deal-breaker.) But I believe, through God's grace and lots of work, that almost any two people can make a relationship work, even through the quirks.

However, as we see from Paul's words in this week's verse, bearing with each other is not just for the sake of having a happy relationship. We humble ourselves and adapt to others with the goal of winning them to Christ. Sure, your significant other may already have a relationship with Jesus, but that doesn't mean they're spiritually mature in every area that you're spiritually mature, and vice versa.

When we humble ourselves and meet our significant other where they're at, we show them the same love that Christ shows us: a love that shows grace before change. It's important to note that Christ does call us to change, but not before forgiveness is already given. If you do notice a quirk in your significant other, it might not even need to change; it really depends on what God's Word says about it. Do your best to cover everything in prayer. Christ may lead you to talk to your significant other about change, or He may give you the grace to bear with them.

PRAYER

Ask God to help you set realistic expectations for your significant other and let go of the ones that may not be so realistic.

Ask God to help you show grace when dealing with personal quirks your significant other may have.

Ask God to remind you to be humble, always remembering your own quirks and imperfections.

Running from Temptation

She caught him by his garment, saying, "Lie with me." But he left his garment in her hand and fled and got out of the house.
—

Genesis 39:12

Back in high school, I knew a girl who started dating a mutual friend of ours. During the beginning of their relationship, her parents were relatively involved and cautious of the new relationship. They asked their daughter to avoid spending any time completely alone with her new boyfriend. Although they didn't have any reason not to trust the couple—both loved the Lord and desired a relationship that was pleasing to Him—they also understood that men and women enter into relationships for a reason: because they're attracted to each other!

So my friend and her boyfriend decided to honor her parents and not spend any time alone with each other. They had a great time going on group dates and hanging out at friends' houses together. If they wanted to have a private conversation, they simply went to a public place and had a discreet conversation there. Their relationship was for the most part drama-free and fun, as they got to know each other better while respecting her parents and honoring God.

After my friend and her boyfriend had been together for about a year, her parents told her that, if she wanted to, she could spend time alone with him, as they figured she and her boyfriend had proven themselves responsible. The couple was excited to be able to have time together without friends or family nearby and, as you might have guessed, took advantage of their newly lengthened leash. Not two months went by before the couple found themselves in intimate situations together and were tempted to have sex outside of marriage.

The couple tried a few times to reform their relationship because, after all, they did want a relationship that was pleasing to God. They tried reading the Bible and praying together more. They tried asking friends to hold them accountable. But ultimately, they found that the temptation to be together intimately was too strong, and they ended up breaking off the relationship altogether.

I could make a list of precautions and safety measures to help you and your significant other avoid my friend's fate, but I'd like to do something else instead. Rather than prescribe topical treatments, let's uncover the issue at the root. You could go down the longest checklist in the world trying to make sure that your relationship meets Christ's standards, but without a real, loving relationship with Him, what's the point?

The way I see it, my friend and her boyfriend, though they still desired a strong relationship with God, allowed their romance to become the most important thing in their life. As a result, they tried to coordinate their relationship with Christ around their relationship with each other, instead of the other way around. If God had been the single most important thing in their life, making smart decisions to avoid the temptation to sin would have been much easier. I'm not saying they wouldn't have been tempted—of course, their attraction to each other would have been the same and their physical desires would have been the same. But their desire to honor Christ and their willingness to put down things that would compromise that honor would have been stronger.

So, while you're reading this, I want you to ask yourself: "Am I living in a way that reflects that God is the most important thing in my life? If not, why not?" Our first priority should always be our relationship with Him.

With that said, there *are* a few smart things you can do with your significant other in order to avoid situations where temptation may get the best of you. Unlike my friends above, try to avoid spending unnecessary time alone. Sure, you're going to want time alone, and you may even be able to handle it, but there's safety in numbers, and avoiding the temptation altogether is better than finding out you couldn't handle it after all. Secondly, find a couple who can hold you accountable. Whether separately or together, be sure you have godly people in your life who want to see your relationship succeed, but also, more importantly, want to see your relationship with Christ grow and mature. Lastly, cover your relationship in prayer and do your best to hold it with an open hand, letting God lead you to the right decisions. God is not against dating couples. Christ uses marriage to be a picture of his relationship with the church and, in our culture, dating and engagement almost always come before marriage. Date your significant other in a way that submits to your relationship to Christ, and you really can't go wrong.

PRAYER

Pray that God would help you and your significant other to hold your relationship with an open hand.

Pray that God would reveal areas of temptation or weakness and give you wisdom for how to handle them or avoid them altogether.

Ask God to bring godly mentors into your lives who can hold you accountable and speak wisdom into your lives.

A Sense of Selfishness

For he who was called in the Lord as a bondservant is a freedman of the Lord. Likewise he who was free when called is a bondservant of Christ. You were bought with a price; do not become bondservants of men.

—

1 Corinthians 7:22–23

There's one human trait that no relationship can ever escape. All we can hope to do is manage it (with help) and try to keep it under control. That trait is selfishness. I'd argue that selfishness ultimately boils down to a sense of entitlement. When we believe that we deserve more than we actually have, it'll start to show in our actions and our attitudes.

Here's an example: On a Saturday morning, I get up and see that the dishes were left out overnight, so I start to wash them. My mood is okay until I see Josh come in, sit on the couch, and start scrolling through his phone. Now I start thinking, *Why doesn't he jump in and help me? Some of these dishes are his, too, after all.*

In looking at this scenario, many people might identify Josh as the selfish one in the story, and yes, he probably is being a little selfish. But let's ask the question: Why does it upset me that I'm washing his dishes? If I'm being extremely honest with myself, it's because I feel entitled, like I shouldn't have to wash anyone's dishes but my own. Like I deserve better than to have to wash my husband's dirty dishes.

The truth is, if I didn't have an entitled attitude, washing someone else's dishes, or doing more than my fair share of work in general, wouldn't be a big deal at all. Because, as a sinner saved by grace, what on earth am I entitled to?

When we have the mind-set that everything we're given is a gift that can be used to glorify God, doing more than our fair share of work can transform itself from a frustrating burden into an opportunity to show our significant other what the sacrificial love of God is truly like. When we're grateful for our ability to give of our own time, our own resources, and our own strength, we're telling God that we're thankful for the gifts he has given us. We're showing Christ we understand that our lives are not our own and that we were bought at a price. (And while this mind-set is extremely meaningful in dating relationships and marriage, it goes without saying that it can also be applied to any relationship, even those with strangers.)

I also want to note that I've found that if we do our best to understand the reason *why* our significant other may have dropped the ball, it helps us relate to them as a fellow imperfect human being, rather than someone who inconveniently messed up. As discussed in week 10 (page 28), if it's easy for us to come up with excuses for why we let our significant other down, we should at the very least make an effort to understand why they let us down from time to time.

Of course, this doesn't always mean you should allow people to take advantage of you. And if your significant other calls themselves a believer, it's okay to hold them to the standards that God sets for us in His Word. That being said, both you and your significant other are imperfect and have naturally selfish tendencies. Every so often, you'll have to do more than your fair share. Likewise, sometimes you're going to drop the ball and your significant other will have to pick up your slack. It may feel frustrating in the moment to the person who's doing more, but if we're able to have a proper, humble view of ourselves, it'll help us be more forgiving toward our partner.

Matthew 7:2 is a good reminder to keep our judgments and grudges in check: "For with the judgment you pronounce you will be judged, and with the measure you use it will be measured to you." So the next time you feel a grumble rising in you because of something your significant other did or didn't do, remember how much you have been forgiven. Remind yourself that Christ took every bit of judgment that you (and your partner) deserved and bore that in your place. What a truly humbling thing to comprehend.

PRAYER

Ask Christ to constantly remind you of how much you have been forgiven.

Ask Christ to help you see yourself with humility and understand that your significant other is an imperfect human being who needs as much grace as you do.

Ask God to show you opportunities where you can be servant-hearted and love your significant other, even when you may not feel they "deserve" it.

Serving God Together

And let us consider how to stir up one another to love and good works, not neglecting to meet together, as is the habit of some, but encouraging one another, and all the more as you see the Day drawing near.
—
Hebrews 10:24–25

In my opinion, one of the biggest possible downfalls in any relationship is selfishness. It's the root cause of many outward problems, and it's extremely dangerous because it comes oh so naturally to every one of us. But selfishness isn't something that happens just to individuals. Couples can be selfish *as couples*, too.

Every couple is different, with their own personalities and tendencies. But I have known many couples who waste much of their relationship on working the jobs they have to work, going to church together when it's expected, and then coming home and spending the rest of their day—and ultimately a large portion of their life—seeking out their own enjoyment, comfort, and entertainment. Of course, every individual and every couple needs some time to rest and recuperate from the strains of daily life. But many waste an enormous opportunity to serve the church in the larger capacity granted to them as believers.

There are three main reasons why I would encourage every couple to serve together.

1. **To develop a sense of selflessness.** As I previously mentioned, every individual, and therefore every couple, will have selfish and self-focused tendencies. If you practice going against those tendencies, habits of selflessness and servant-heartedness will inevitably begin to move in you. Of course, people can end up serving begrudgingly and without the right attitude. But if you seek out opportunities to serve with a gracious heart and a love for God and others, your intentions will always be in the right place.

2. **To set an example for others.** Whether or not you and your significant other get married one day and have children, you will always have the opportunity to set an example for others. Serve the church together out of love for God, and you'll inspire others to do the same. If you want to raise children who know Christ and love others, the best way to teach them is to show them what an overflow of Christ's love looks like in real life.

3. **To use your time on earth wisely.** If you can't think of any other reason to serve with your significant other, do it because Christ told you to. James 1:27 says, "Religion that is pure and undefiled before God the Father, is this: to visit orphans and widows in their affliction, and to keep oneself unstained from the world." We will be held accountable for how we loved and served others during our time here on earth. So, if for no other reason, serve others so you have evidence of your faith that you can reflect on throughout your life.

It's my sincere belief that the more we give with an open hand, the easier it becomes to give. When we realize that our time here on earth is itself a gift from God and that the biggest purpose our lives can serve is to bring glory to Him, spending time serving others with your partner makes a whole lot of sense. Of course, serving individually is also great and will probably at times be necessary; depending on your schedules and unique gifts, one of you may be able to serve more than the other, or your needs may be called upon in different capacities.

Although serving will use more of your time and energy, you and your significant other will feel more fulfilled and have a stronger sense of purpose for your relationship if you find ways to serve together or in coordination with each other.

PRAYER

Pray that God would open your eyes to needs within your church and/or community where you would be a great fit to jump in and begin serving.

Ask God to give you the wisdom to know when to serve and know when to rest.

Ask that God would allow you and your significant other to have an eternal mind-set and hold the things in your life with an open hand.

Learning Each Other's Language

Though I am free and belong to no one, I have made myself a slave to everyone, to win as many as possible.
—

1 Corinthians 9:19 (NIV)

You may be familiar with *The Five Love Languages* by Gary Chapman, which lays out five ways people are naturally inclined to give and receive love: words of affirmation, quality time, receiving gifts, acts of service, and physical touch. When I first read the book and took the accompanying personality test, I discovered that my love languages were words of affirmation and physical touch (although now that I'm a mother, they've evolved into words of affirmation and acts of service). I asked Josh to take the test and discovered that his love languages were quality time and physical touch, which has more or less stayed the same.

Regardless of whether you take the test yourself or whether you find Chapman's framework helpful, this week's devotion is about how to interpret the signs that your significant other is trying their best to show you love, and how you in turn can show them love in the way that's most meaningful to them.

For example, this is a situation that often happens in our home: I walk into a kitchen of dirty dishes. I might feel annoyed that Josh left his dishes out, but because I want to show him love, I begin to do the dishes and accept that sometimes in relationships we do more than our fair share of the work. Josh notices I'm frustrated, and in an effort to make things better, gives me a long hug and asks me to sit with him for a while, because that's his way of communicating love. But my frustration digs in deeper—I'm trying to show him I love him by cleaning *his* mess, and now he's getting in the way of that? I tell him I'm busy and keep going in my efforts to "love" him, and we both feel misunderstood and frustrated.

It's in moments like these that I need to stop and realize that Josh, in his way, is trying to remind me that he loves me. On the flip side, Josh often has to make an effort to remember that he can show me love via acts of service, like doing the dishes before I get to them.

In what areas might your partner be trying to show you love that you may not realize? Are you getting frustrated by trying to show them love in ways they might not recognize? Once you've determined how your significant other feels and shows love, it's important to *pay attention*. It can be easy to forget that your significant other may be *showing* love in a way that's different from how you typically *feel* loved.

If you do something that your significant other seems to really appreciate, do it again—and then think of ways you can expand on that. If your significant other feels love when you're just spending time with them, make an effort to set aside time for simply being with them. If they feel love through words of affirmation, try to make a habit of writing notes or sending encouraging texts from time to time. What might feel like small but intentional changes will let you reap the benefit of a happy and fulfilled significant other, and who doesn't want that?

Lastly, if you feel your significant other isn't really speaking your love language (whether you're using Chapman's definitions or not), try having an honest conversation about what makes you feel loved. Then, if your partner does make an effort to speak your love language, be sure to recognize it, remember it, and thank them for it.

PRAYER

Ask God to remind you that different people feel love in different ways.

Ask God to give you a heart of humility and help you be flexible in learning how to show love in the ways that others feel it.

Ask God to help you remember the times that your significant other has shown you love in the past, so it becomes easier to forgive frustrating moments in the future.

The Comparison Trap

"For the pagans run after all these things, and your heavenly Father knows that you need them. But seek first his kingdom and his righteousness, and all these things will be given to you as well."

—

Matthew 6:32–33 (NIV)

When you're sitting in a doctor's office or riding in the passenger seat of a car, what are you doing? I would be willing to bet my next Starbucks coffee that you're scrolling through your phone, probably on a social media app. I do it, too. If I were to add up the minutes I spend scrolling through social media, it would probably equal a substantial portion of my day. And the worst part is that I spend so much of that time comparing myself to others.

My social media platform of choice is typically Instagram, where I scroll through pictures of women with cleaner homes who travel the world in fabulous clothes. This can go for romantic relationships, too; it can be easy to see perfectly staged photos of another couple's glamorous date night and feel like your relationship, with all its imperfections, can't compete. Of course, comparison doesn't take place only as we scroll through social media. It can happen anywhere, even in our own churches. Have you ever been jealous of the person who always seemed to have a more cheerful attitude than you? Or the person who was asked to lead the Bible study instead of you?

Comparison isn't a one-way street. How often do we post something on social media that portrays our life as some sort of picturesque walk through the park? Do we ever secretly hope that people feel a tinge of jealousy as they hit the Like button? And what for? Often, when we post something that represents a more ideal or polished version of our lives, we're doing so to feel validated or accepted by people we likely don't even know or interact with. But in caring enough about what others think or becoming jealous when we realize we don't have what someone else has, we are showing that our treasure is not stored up in heaven, but here on earth. And, as Jesus says in Matthew 6:21 (NIV), "Where your treasure is, there your heart will be also."

In my experience, the more freely we give of ourselves, our resources, and our time, and the more open our hearts are to loving others, the less we compare ourselves with others. If I see someone on social media, wonder where they are in their relationship with Christ, and feel compassion for them, my notion that they might have a nicer home than I do becomes irrelevant. How much less likely would we be to show off the highlights of our lives on social media if we remembered that many others are struggling through their own circumstances? Why would we try to compare someone else's marriage or dating relationship to ours, when we could instead focus on a deeper understanding of and gratitude for the relationship God has given us?

What we need to understand is that we have the ability to use our relationships, including the ones we maintain through social media, to form like-minded communities in which people build each other up. When we compare our lives to those of friends or strangers, we have to remember that what we see and what people tell us will never be the full story—you never know what someone may be dealing with in secret or be too embarrassed to share. More importantly, God gave us our lives, our circumstances, and our individual stories for a purpose. Remember that your specific story can reach people in a way that others' can't. You can use your story to point people to Christ in a way that no one else can! Be thankful for the story *you're* living. Use it to build up the people around you and encourage them in their faith.

PRAYER

Ask God to remind you to ponder the soul of the person you usually feel jealous of, and to help you feel compassion for them and pray for them.

Ask God to help you and your significant other use your stories, individually and together, to build community and point others to Christ.

Pray that both you and your significant other would run full force toward Christ and, having your eyes set on Him, let go of any comparison and jealousy you once held on to.

A Mature Relationship

[Until] we all attain to the unity of the faith and of the knowledge of the Son of God, to mature manhood ... we may no longer be children, tossed to and fro by the waves and carried about by every wind of doctrine. ... Rather, speaking the truth in love, we are to grow up in every way into him who is the head, into Christ.

—

Ephesians 4:13–15

How mature do you feel your relationship is? In my experience, there's a pretty straightforward way to tell whether a relationship shows maturity or, well ... not. All you have to do is look at how a couple handles conflict. Any level of conflict, really.

Say you send your significant other a text in the morning, but they don't respond until the afternoon. When they do respond, do you wait several hours to text back to give them a taste of how it feels? Or perhaps you've gotten into a fight where both of you said things that you probably shouldn't have. Knowing you weren't the only one in the wrong, how long does it take before you apologize? Do you wait it out until your significant other apologizes first?

In relationships, we often tend to overcomplicate things. I've talked to many men and women in relationships, and they often ask what I think their significant other meant when they said such-and-such, or what they should say to avoid hurting their partner's feelings.

For some reason, our go-to mind-set is that we need to rack our minds to find some complicated hidden message in our significant other's words, or concoct some sort of response that's better than the truth.

To questions like these, I always respond, "Try asking them to clarify what they mean. Just let them know you're trying to get on the same page." Or "Why don't you try telling them your situation? Let them know what you're dealing with and the thought process behind your decision." In most cases, as I mentioned in weeks 1 (page 1) and 15 (page 43), I've found that overexplaining helps avoid misunderstandings and clarifies the intentions behind our actions.

In the moment, it can often feel more pleasant to beat around the bush, preserve feelings, or "save face." And while there's definitely something to be said for using *tact* in sensitive situations, that's not the same thing as being passive aggressive or being dishonest. Using tact means being sensitive and caring for others' feelings, which are both things that you can do while having an honest and direct conversation.

Practicing grace in situations of conflict and confrontation will always show a mature faith. When you come into a situation of conflict with your significant other, ask yourself what would be the most grace-filled but direct and honest way to handle the situation. Remember, showing grace does not always mean accepting someone's behavior. As Paul says in Romans 6:1–2, "What shall we say then? Are we to continue in sin that grace may abound? By no means! How can we who died to sin still live in it?" But as Christ calls us out of our sin, He also continues to show grace as we, inevitably, fail from time to time.

PRAYER

Ask God to remind you to show grace during times of conflict and disappointment.

If you struggle with being direct and honest, pray for God to reveal ways to be direct with each other while keeping feelings in mind.

In the future, when facing a situation where confrontation will be necessary, before you say anything, ask God to prepare the heart of the person you'll be speaking to. Sometimes, God may work to review the sin with them, without any additional effort needed on your part.

Taking Time to Rest

And on the seventh day God finished his work that he had done, and he rested on the seventh day from all his work that he had done. So God blessed the seventh day and made it holy, because on it God rested from all his work that he had done in creation.

—

Genesis 2:2–3

When you're single, life can often feel hectic, with responsibilities from work, school, volunteering, ministry, family, and many other aspects. Not to mention the things you do for fun! Combine that with the schedule of another person, and now you're coordinating how to actually do life together. Josh and I have sometimes felt as though the only time we had for each other at the end of the day was to give each other a high five, provide a quick rundown of our day and what we had planned for the next day, and then go to sleep so the whole thing could start over. There may be times in your relationship when you feel the same.

While busy stages of life will often be inevitable, they should, in fact, be *stages*. When you begin to join lives with another person, your schedule will only become more demanding—*much* more demanding if you end up getting married and having kids. No matter the case, you and your significant other will need to develop habits of "retreat." When you find yourself rushing from one thing to the next, or just consistently exhausted by the end of the day, it may be time to ask yourself if there's anything you can cut back on. A friend of mine who seems to have a constantly packed schedule was recently asked what she does when she starts to feel overwhelmed, and her response was that she grabs her calendar and cancels as many things as possible. (That, and she eats a pint of ice cream.)

Follow her advice at your own risk, but I think there's something to be said for the fact that so much on our schedule actually *is* cancelable. Oftentimes, busyness feels like something we're forced into because we get the sense things will fall apart without us, but that's not always the case. Sure, your church may need more volunteers in its outreach ministry, but that doesn't mean that *you* personally have to volunteer *right now*. Don't get me wrong, it's important to be involved with and serve in your church (see week 21, page 61), but if you're already volunteering in other ministries, or if you're in a stage of life that's demanding too much of you in another area, it's okay to say no to adding another commitment.

While you're policing your own commitments and making time for rest, there may also come a day when you need to help your significant other do the same. If you notice they're committing to too much and seem overwhelmed, you may need to step in and suggest they try to cut a thing or two from their schedule. If they can't, helping them take time to rest, even for a short while, can make all the difference. This may even mean spending a short time away from each other if necessary.

Jesus really does give us the best example when it comes to taking time to get away and rest. Anyone could argue that He was extremely needed at all times, but even so, the Bible often mentions the times when, just for a while, He separated himself, prayed, and rested. A great example of this is when He was with His disciples in a boat on the sea of Galilee: "There arose a great storm on the sea, so that the boat was being swamped by the waves; but he was asleep. And they went and woke him, saying, 'Save us, Lord; we are perishing.' And he said to them, 'Why are you afraid, O you of little faith?' Then he rose and rebuked the winds and the sea, and there was a great calm" (Matthew 8:24–26).

Of course Jesus knew that when the storm came, His disciples would be scared and looking for Him, but He also knew how the story would end. So He rested. When it was His time, He got up and helped His disciples, but not before. In the same way, do your best to be discerning about how and when you're really needed, and when it's okay to simply rest.

PRAYER

Ask God to watch over your schedule so you don't busy yourself to the point of burnout, whether in work, ministry, social life, or any other area.

Ask God to bless your time of rest and use it to bring you closer to Him and renew your mind and body.

Ask God to give you the ability to say no sometimes and perhaps bring in other capable people to fill the role you declined.

Don't Compete, Coordinate

Having gifts that differ according to the grace given to us, let us use them: if prophecy, in proportion to our faith; if service, in our serving; the one who teaches, in his teaching; the one who exhorts, in his exhortation; the one who contributes, in generosity; the one who leads, with zeal; the one who does acts of mercy, with cheerfulness.
—

Romans 12:6–8

In your relationship, you'll find that you and your partner have different strengths and weaknesses. That being the case, you're going to come at various situations with different perspectives and opinions on how to handle them—which, at times, might very well drive you nuts.

Let's say you and your significant other are in the car and having a conversation about a friend who seems to be making bad choices. Let's also say you have the spiritual gift of mercy, while your significant other has the spiritual gift of teaching. You feel your friend really needs someone who will listen to them, understand them, and show sympathy toward their situation—in short, that someone will be able to "love" them into making better choices. On the flip side, your partner feels strongly that your friend needs to be warned that their choices are unwise and confronted about the poor decisions they're making. Once this friend sees how their behavior leads to bad outcomes, they'll have no alternative but to pick a wiser path.

It's clear how the two halves of this couple, with very different spiritual gifts, might butt heads during this conversation. One prefers less confrontation and more compassion. The other prefers a direct "talking to" that clearly outlines how different choices would result in more positive outcomes. Which approach is better?

Sure, while reading a devotional, it's easy to say that all gifts can work together, but in the moment, it might not be so easy to believe. You, with the spiritual gift of mercy, may grumble to yourself (or out loud to your significant other) that their way of handling situations is too confrontational and doesn't show enough compassion. After all, Christ showed compassion all the time to those caught in sin. Your partner, with the spiritual gift of teaching, might point out that if all we ever showed was compassion, no one would ever change for the better. A third person who had the spiritual gift of service might criticize both those approaches, saying we would do better to serve those in need, showing the wayward friend by example the best way to make choices.

What God understands when calling each one of us to Himself is that we are all different. We can all look at the same situation and come up with many different ways to handle it, all for the glory of God. Paul, when writing his letter to the Roman church, also knew that we have a tendency to think of our way as the best way, which is why I believe he felt it important to include "I say to everyone among you not to think of himself more highly than he ought to think" (Romans 12:3).

We are encouraged to use the gifts that were given to each of us, and I think that includes validating the gifts of the believers around us as well. You may prefer to teach others a new or better way of doing things, but the gift of mercy may show itself to be more useful in other situations. As much as you may prefer (or even have a tendency to take pride in) your own gifts, do your best to remember the validity and importance of the other gifts God has given to those around you.

If you become frustrated with your significant other's preferred way of handling situations, try to find a common ground where all of your gifts work together for the best possible outcome: the one that honors Christ the most. If two very different people can come together and coordinate their differences for the sake of the Gospel, that is where Christ receives the most glory from us.

If you're unsure about the spiritual gifts you were given, that's okay! Take time to pray and do some research and self-evaluation to see where your tendencies lie. (Of course, if you feel you have the spiritual gift of exhortation, that doesn't necessarily mean you'll never be called to prophecy, just like those with the spiritual gift of teaching will have to hold their tongue and show mercy from time to time.) Once you have a better idea of what your spiritual gifts may be, talk about them with your significant other. Discuss ways you can use your gifts together rather than in competition with each other. Then, going forward, do your best to remember the gifts your partner has been blessed with and allow them to use *their* specific gifts for the glory of God in coordination with yours.

PRAYER

Pray that God would reveal to each of you the strengths and gifts He's blessed you with.

Ask that God would allow you and your significant other to work together in harmony, each using your own gifts and respecting the other's, for God's glory.

Realistic Expectations

"So whatever you wish that others would do to you, do also to them."
—

Matthew 7:12

When I was young, I wrote a list of qualities I wanted my future husband to have. He was definitely going to be kind and handsome (check and check), love sports (check), and want kids (check). Then, as I got older, I read a few love stories and watched *A Walk to Remember*, and the list got a little bit longer. My future husband, I decided, would definitely never be the type of person to get frustrated or angry with me. He would always take the time to plan romantic dates, and we would take every opportunity we had to sit out under the stars and talk about our love for each other.

Safe to say, I was going to be waiting a while to check those boxes. Not that my husband isn't romantic or that he's constantly huffing and puffing in anger, but somewhere along the line, life happens. People end up being more human than you expect them to be.

The phenomenon of unrealistic expectations isn't confined to women wishing their boyfriends would be more like the ones in Nicholas Sparks books. It happens with men, too, though often in a different way. Through my work as a blogger, I've spoken with many men who don't understand why their wives aren't as playful or happy as they used to be, or why they stopped "taking care of themselves" the way they did when they were 20. (What they don't mention is how many nights in a row their wives have been up all night with their new baby.)

Overall, as men and women, we have high expectations of each other. Whether we're waiting for them to change or hoping they'll *never* change, many of us end up jaded and confused as to why our significant other is not the way we thought they'd be. You might even start wondering if every relationship is like this, or if it's just yours. You might wonder if you chose the wrong person because they didn't end up being how you imagined.

The thing is, there's nothing wrong with the person. There's something wrong with those kinds of expectations.

This can become especially clear when we examine whether we hold ourselves to our own expectations. We might get upset because our significant other rarely plans romantic dates for us, but usually we don't ask ourselves about the last time we planned a romantic date for them. We might feel frustrated if our boyfriend or girlfriend has a hard time forgiving us quickly when we didn't *mean* to hurt them, but how often do we hold on to grudges after they've apologized for something they did wrong?

Often, our negative emotions toward our significant other tell us what our expectations actually are, even if we never intended to have them. When that happens, we need to ask ourselves if we're willing to hold ourselves to our own expectations. If you want your significant other to forgive you quickly, are you also going to forgive them quickly? If you want them to be patient with you when you make mistakes, do you also bear with them when they make mistakes? If you want them to be the type of person who is self-sacrificial and eager to serve, are you first setting that example for them? If you *do* usually meet your own expectations and don't understand why your partner can't do the same, remember that it's important for all of us to measure our expectations against Christ's. We all fall short.

You may simply need to accept your partner as they are and do your best to appreciate the gifts and unique qualities they bring to your relationship. If your significant other is into sports and you can't imagine sitting through a whole football game, why not make the effort for them? If they appreciate romantic gestures, why not go out of your way to buy them flowers once in a while? If your girlfriend or boyfriend tends to be more analytical, emotional, bubbly, or serious than you pictured them being, do your best to learn from and appreciate that quality instead of wishing they were more like you or the person you had hoped them to be. In the end, understand that God made you differently and gave you diverse gifts that can all be used for His glory.

PRAYER

Ask God to help you manage your expectations and evaluate whether or not they're realistic.

Ask God to allow you to have grace toward your significant other in areas where they may not meet the expectations you once had.

Ask God to open your eyes to areas where you may not be living up to reasonable expectations.

Guarding Your Heart

Keep your heart with all vigilance, for from it flow the springs of life.
—

Proverbs 4:23

In high school and especially at a Christian university, I often heard the term "guard your heart." At the time, I wasn't really sure what "guarding my heart" actually looked like, and I wasn't sure I wanted in. I wanted to date guys! Guarding my heart sounded safe but also pretty boring. Was I supposed to just shun anyone who asked me out on a date? And if I did go on a date, was I supposed to be some sort of mysterious and private person who kept my personal life to myself? And why was it always we girls who were told to guard their hearts? Were men some kind of evil heart-snatchers we needed to be afraid of?

The concept of guarding my heart seemed abstract and confusing, to say the least. But the more I dug into what it meant and the reasons it appeared in the Bible, the more I realized it was less like a recommendation and more like a safeguard. Another version of the verse above reads, "Above all else, guard your heart, for everything you do flows from it" (Proverbs 4:23 NIV). Just like the idiom," What goes up must come down," the things we allow into our hearts must eventually pour out. So it makes sense to be cautious about what those things are.

I've known many young Christians who enter into relationships with nonbelievers. Either they assume that their boyfriend or girlfriend will eventually become saved under their influence, or they choose not to care and push thoughts of future discord to the back of their mind. However, almost every person I've known to date a nonbeliever has also grown stagnant in their faith. What they allowed their heart to love reproduced itself in their own life.

Of course, we don't just see this in relationships. We also see it with the love of money or material things, the love of recognition, the love of being accepted. If these are the things we allow ourselves to love and place high value on, our habits and behaviors will be shaped by them.

So the concept of guarding your heart is twofold. First, it means only giving your heart to those whose hearts also belong to Jesus; if the person you give your heart to already belongs to Jesus, then your heart can be found right where you want it to be! Second, it means honest self-evaluation about how much you value things that are not of Christ. Colossians 3:3–5 says, "For you have died, and your life is hidden with Christ in God. When Christ who is your life appears, then you also will appear with him in glory. Put to death therefore what is earthly in you: sexual immorality, impurity, passion, evil desire, and covetousness, which is idolatry."

Be honest with yourself and your significant other about the things you may be allowing into your hearts that don't glorify God. If you allow yourself to value fashion and your appearance too highly, are you talking with your peers about that instead of building each other up in your faith? Does watching sports occupy almost all your free time rather than a small portion of it, so you don't have time to perform any ministry? Of course, it's not wrong to buy a beautiful pair of shoes or talk about last night's game. But these things, like anything, can be idolized. And when they are, we often find ourselves overconsuming them and, as a result, letting them overflow into the rest of our lives.

So, yes, guard your heart. Examine the value you put on people and things other than Christ. Be cautious, so that what you allow into your heart will produce only things that glorify God.

PRAYER

Ask that God would reveal to you the things in your life that you may be valuing more highly than you should.

Ask God if there are areas in your life where you could be more cautious and take better care to guard your heart.

Ask God to help you safeguard your significant other's heart as well—not controlling them, but praying for them and making suggestions to them when God leads you to.

A Healthy View of Sex

And the man and his wife were both naked and were not ashamed.
—

Genesis 2:25

Depending on the community you each grew up in, you and your partner may have very different ideas about the topic of sex. It seems as though the mainstream secular community blasts us with pictures and talk of sex as a casual and everyday part of life even for those who are not married. Or perhaps you grew up in a community where talking about sex was taboo, sex was seen as a dirty act, and the thought of enjoying it was a big no-no. Whichever the case, I want to tell you that there is hope and there is balance.

To be frank: God created sex. He made sex before there was any sin in the world. Consider that for a minute. God believed sex to be good. He was well aware that Adam and Eve would have sex. It didn't come as a surprise to Him—He planned it. And for whatever reason, God made sex enjoyable. He didn't have to; sex could have just been a means to procreate and nothing more.

So why did God give us sex? And why did he choose to make it enjoyable? To answer those questions, let's start with a different question. What's the purpose of marriage?

Like all things God made, marriage was created to bring Him glory. God designed marriage very specifically to be a picture of

Christ's relationship to the church. And Christ doesn't want just any old relationship with His church. He wants an intimate and enjoyable relationship with His church. The more we as the church enjoy Christ, the more glory He gets. So if a marriage is a picture of Jesus Christ and His church, and Jesus wants that relationship to be intimate and enjoyable, then of course he made intimacy between husbands and wives to be enjoyable also!

I am telling you this because I want you to have a healthy view of sex throughout your dating relationships and into your marriage. I've heard from many Christian couples that they struggled early on in their marriages because for many years they heard that sex was sinful or else sex just wasn't spoken of at all. And many dating couples react differently to this. Some will turn their minds completely off to sex in order to block it out and stay "safe." Others will be confused, wondering why God made sex enjoyable if they aren't allowed to enjoy it.

When you're dating, it's okay to look forward to a healthy and loving sexual relationship with your future spouse. Sex is a gift from God, but like all of God's gifts, it can be used to glorify Him or it can be abused. The fact that food tastes good and is pleasurable to eat is a gift from God, but we can abuse that gift by being gluttonous.

If you're reading this book, you probably fall into one of three categories: those who have had sex outside the security of marriage, those who are still working toward saving sex for marriage, and those who have an unhealthy fear of sex. Or you may be caught somewhere in between. Maybe you have had sex with a partner in the past but have since decided to keep sex for marriage, or perhaps you are a survivor of sexual assault or abuse, and are struggling to have a healthy view of God-glorifying sex. I want to let you know that whatever your past experience with sex, God does make all things new again. For those who are united in Christ, there is always hope for love and redemption. I write this because I don't want you to fear sex in your future marriage. As 1 John 4:18 says, "There is no fear in love, but perfect love casts out fear."

PRAYER

Ask God to give you wisdom and discernment in a sex-saturated culture.

Ask God to help you and your significant other put boundaries in place to help you steer clear of sexual temptation.

Ask that God would allow you to have a healthy view of sex and understand how a sexual relationship, within marriage, can be glorifying to God.

True Generosity

One gives freely, yet grows all the richer; another withholds what he should give, and only suffers want. Whoever brings blessing will be enriched, and one who waters will himself be watered.

—

Proverbs 11:24–25

We often look at generosity as something we'll be able to do at some point in the future. Someday, when life settles down, when we've gained control of our finances and we have more to give, then we'll give more freely. Someday, when we have more time on our hands, then we'll spend more time serving.

But the Bible consistently shows us that generosity is not about the amount of time spent serving or the amount of money we're able to give. Generosity is an attitude of the heart. Generosity is a desire to give, no matter how much we have to begin with. Think of the poor widow in Mark 12 who only gives two copper coins to the church, while many rich people donate much more. Jesus tells His disciples that she has actually given more than anyone else because "they all contributed out of their abundance, but she out of her poverty has put in everything she had" (Mark 12:44).

Generosity and giving is also something we should be able to feel, something that makes us trust that God is in control of our finances in the first place. The motives behind our giving make a big impact on how the gift is received by God. The widow in the story above trusted the Lord to provide what she needed, while the rich people gave with the intention of being seen as wealthy or generous. But as Christ points out, He is fully aware of our motives when we give.

Do we give out of our own abundance so that our giving doesn't require any faith in God to provide for us? Do we give in order to feel like "good Christians"? Or do we earnestly give out of a desire for our gifts to be used for the sake of the Gospel, like the Macedonian church that Paul said "gave according to their means . . . and beyond their means, of their own accord, begging us earnestly for the favor of taking part in the relief of the saints" (2 Corinthians 8:3–4).

Paul rejoices in these gifts because he understands that the members of that church are building up for themselves treasures in heaven, as Jesus instructs: "Do not lay up for yourselves treasures on earth . . . but lay up for yourselves treasures in heaven, where neither moth nor rust destroys and where thieves do not break in and steal. For where your treasure is, there your heart will be also" (Matthew 6:19–21). The things we save up for and enjoy here on this earth will only be able to make us happy temporarily. By being generous with our earthly gifts, we're saying that our hope is not here on earth, but in our eternal life with Christ. Our life with Christ far surpasses any temporary joy in this life.

What acts of generosity can you and your significant other perform together? If you're starting to talk about marriage and combining finances, how will you build generosity into your budget? If you find yourself struggling to be generous with what you have, remind each other that God does not judge the amount you give. God looks at your heart—where you are putting your hope and what your intentions are in giving.

PRAYER

Ask that God open your eyes to opportunities to give of your time and money.

Ask that God would allow you to give with a joyful heart and hold your time and money with an open hand.

Ask that God would teach you to rely on Him and allow your finances to be a reflection of your hope in a future with Him.

Quick to Hear, Slow to Speak

Know this, my beloved brothers: let every person be quick to hear, slow to speak, slow to anger; for the anger of man does not produce the righteousness of God.

—

James 1:19–20

One of the things I like to tell couples (and myself, and my husband) is that there are usually two ways to respond to conflict: escalation or de-escalation.

Fights usually happen when we're offended by or frustrated with someone, when it becomes extremely easy to let our emotions dictate our tone and the words we use. Let's say your significant other chooses to spend several nights in a row with his or her friends instead of spending time with you. When our emotions are running high, we're bound to say things we wouldn't normally say. You might be tempted to say something along the lines of, "Why are you being so thoughtless? Don't you care about me?" or use generalizing sentences like "You never make time for me!" or "You only care about your friends!" Your partner's natural response will be to become defensive, and before you know it, you're fighting.

But there is a better alternative, and that's having a conversation—listening earnestly and speaking honestly.

I like to practice using a give-take statement in order to let the person I'm upset with know how I feel, but remind them that I still respect them as a person. I'll use Josh in an example: "Josh, I know you haven't seen your friends in a while, but you haven't spent time with me a single night this week. Do you think you could make some time for us tonight or tomorrow?" Here, I'm letting Josh know that I've thought about why he might be doing what he's doing (I understand he hasn't seen his friends in a while), but I also let him know that it's beginning to bother me. Then, I suggest a solution that I feel is fair, and if he agrees, we can both spend our evening happily together. By showing that you understand there's a reason behind your significant other's actions, you're already helping them feel understood rather than judged or attacked. This will help keep them from feeling defensive and ultimately (hopefully) keep the discussion from turning into a heated argument.

Another great way to have a conversation with your partner about something you're unhappy with is to first ask a question. The trick here is doing it in a sincere way and actually trying to understand where your significant other is coming from. Spending time in prayer and in God's Word before you start a discussion will help you have an earnest and forgiving heart before any words are even exchanged. Take time to remind yourself just how much you have been forgiven and how patient the Lord is with you on a daily basis.

Once you've asked your significant other questions that try to get to the bottom of their actions (without sounding as though you're interrogating them), this will be the time when you have to listen. Allow them to explain the reasons and thoughts behind their actions. After that, you might be on the same page, or you might still feel a sense of frustration; these conversations won't always end in agreement. You may have to take it a step further and talk about ways that you and your significant other can compromise and find a solution for your frustration.

In any case, it's extremely important to be honest about how you feel, all the while remembering to be slow to anger, slow to speak, and quick to listen. This might even mean separating yourself from the situation for a little while so you have time to pray over it and ask Christ to give you a godly attitude toward it. But after you've prayed, address it in a timely manner. Don't wait a week to bring up something to your significant other. More often than not, instead of feeling appreciative, they'll feel blindsided and surprised that you were upset at all.

In the end, your goal should be one of restoration and unity. Ask yourself if your words will help you reach that goal. That's not to say that confrontation will always be comfortable. Confrontation can be hard and very uncomfortable at times. But the goal should always be to reconcile and to be unified in Christ. These hard situations will come up in almost any relationship. What makes all the difference is dating someone who truly loves God and understands that we should always be seeking to improve and be more like Him. That, and the fact that, in our journey to do so, we often fail and need forgiveness. If you and your significant other can both agree on those points, and agree to strive for a relationship that brings glory to God, then you'll always be able to work through your fights and disagreements.

PRAYER

Ask that God would give you a humble attitude when it comes to confronting your significant other.

Ask God to remind you to be slow to anger, slow to speak, and quick to listen.

Pray that God would help you and your significant other desire to be unified as brothers and sisters in Christ whose goal is ultimately to bring God glory in everything you do.

Go Deeper

For the body does not consist of one member but of many. If the foot should say, "Because I am not a hand, I do not belong to the body," that would not make it any less a part of the body. And if the ear should say, "Because I am not an eye, I do not belong to the body," that would not make it any less a part of the body. If the whole body were an eye, where would be the sense of hearing? If the whole body were an ear, where would be the sense of smell?
—

1 Corinthians 12:14–17

In your own relationship, have you ever looked at your significant other and wondered why they made a certain decision or why they always seem to do certain things differently than you? Maybe you've wondered why they seem to be perpetually pessimistic or optimistic, or they either don't like going to parties or are always dragging you to a party you'd rather skip.

One of the things that Josh and I love to do in our spare time is take personality tests. Besides finding out which character from *The Office* we are or where our ideal place to live would be, we also like getting deeper into traits that make up the fundamentals of our personalities—things like whether we're more analytical or emotional, introverted or extroverted, factual or intuitive. By getting deeper with each other and doing our best to understand our personalities and inclinations, Josh and I have essentially been able to create a window into the "why" behind many of our actions.

For example, several times we've found ourselves in situations where one of our friends is telling us a story. In that person's story, the teller is always extremely rational and reasonable, and the other person involved is simply "crazy" (or so the story would make it seem). In situations like this, my tendency is to take our friend's story at face value and assume that everything they told us was accurate, because what reason would they have to lie? On the other hand, being on the pessimistic and analytical side, Josh's first reaction is to ask questions. Is the other person in the story *really* as bad as our friend is making it seem? Could there be actually two very different sides of the story?

Of course, having such different personalities has led to some misunderstandings and disagreements in the past. But by taking the time to roll back the layers of each of our personalities and striving to understand each other on a deeper level, we have both come to appreciate the other's qualities and how they complement our own. In doing so, we've actually been able to learn from each other in many ways. I've seen analytical Josh become a more empathetic person who now tries harder to understand the feelings of those around him. And I've learned the habit of asking questions and thinking more critically about the things I hear.

By reading books, taking personality tests (if you enjoy them), and/or simply asking each other questions, you and your significant other will not only learn a great deal about each other, but you'll also learn about yourselves as well. Understanding your own personality gives you the opportunity to figure out what sets you apart from others. It could be that you're the only introvert in an extrovert-dominated office, or, in a family full of creatives, you're the process-oriented, analytical one. Whatever the case, understanding your own personality and the personalities of those around you can help you discover how you can best fit in with others. This is a far better approach than just wondering why you're not like the people around you and trying to adopt behavior that doesn't come naturally.

In my relationship with Josh, I used to wonder why he wasn't more empathetic, and he used to wonder why I wasn't more of a critical thinker. In the end, once we took the time to learn more about our own and each other's personal tendencies and inclinations, we could appreciate the differences in each other. We started to see those differences as opportunities to learn from each other instead of wondering why the other person wasn't more like ourself.

There may come a time when you feel frustrated with the tendencies and inclinations of your significant other. When that day comes, do your best to see how your personality can complement your significant other's personality. After you do this, take some time to be introspective. What are areas where you could personally grow? Saying something like "I'm just that type of person" is never an excuse to keep up problematic behavior forever. We should always be striving to grow and mature.

PRAYER

Ask that God would help you have a deeper understanding of both yourself and your significant other.

When you start to question why your significant other does things a certain way, ask God to remind you how their unique traits can complement your own.

Ask God to give you confidence in your differences and understand how to use your unique traits to better serve the people around you.

Intentional Encouragement

Therefore encourage one another and build one another up,
just as you are doing.
—

1 Thessalonians 5:11

Has someone ever criticized you for something you did, whether intentionally or unintentionally, and their words stuck with you the entire day? What about when someone let you know you were doing a good job? How long did you retain those words? While criticism and encouragement will affect certain people more than others, every person, no matter how emotionally stable they seem, needs encouragement from time to time. Likewise, even those who seem like they wouldn't give it a second thought usually don't *enjoy* hearing criticism.

I remember a time when Josh and I were dating and he tried to do something simple but nice for me, but we had gotten into a small argument and I was critical of him. The next thing I knew, I heard a sniff. Even though he wouldn't make eye contact, I could see the smallest amount of water welling at his tear line, and I knew I had crossed a line. He had tried, I had been critical, and this time it was just a little too much. Once I got past a moment of shock, I immediately felt horrible and wished that I could eat my words. But of course, I couldn't.

As you grow in your relationship with your significant other, you're going to see things that make you raise an eyebrow, scratch your head, or even roll your eyes. And, sure, it's okay to say something, but *the way* you say it can make all the difference. Even the timing of when you choose to say it can make a big difference in the way your significant other receives your feedback. Perhaps you're at a social gathering and you mention you've been trying to watch what you eat, to which your significant other says, "Yeah, except for that date you had with Ben and Jerry's last night." Although it might feel like lighthearted joking, the act of scrutinizing or undermining your significant other, especially in front of a group, can be extremely hurtful. If you've ever been in this situation, I don't need to explain to you the humiliation that someone can feel when they're publicly brought low. Shaming anyone's body, even in jest, is not okay.

Instead, make it a habit to talk up your significant other, whether privately or publicly. Even if it feels like joking, a put-down can be extremely humiliating to anyone, while a small brag here and there can stick with your significant other for days. Even if they're not around, practice saying nice things about your significant other to people. Then it may happen again out of habit when they are with you. Hearing that your partner approves of you and thinks highly of you can be wonderfully encouraging to anyone and ultimately make them feel very loved.

In the end, a habit of encouraging and speaking well of your significant other will come from having a positive mind-set. If your mind constantly goes to thinking about your significant other's failures and the things they do that frustrate you, it will eventually overflow into your words. But when you're able to have a mind-set of gratefulness that acknowledges the things your partner does well, that will also show itself in your words. Do your best to let your partner know when you notice that they've done something well or when they've made a sacrifice that you appreciate. It will help make your significant other feel loved and valued.

PRAYER

Ask that God would help you easily remember the things you appreciate about your significant other and easily forget the things you don't.

Ask God to help you have a spirit of gratefulness and recognize when your partner does something well.

Ask God to give you and your significant other a positive mind-set that focuses on the good rather than the bad.

Prayer Before Action

"Therefore I tell you, whatever you ask for in prayer, believe that you have received it, and it will be yours."
—
Mark 11:24

Many of you are probably familiar with the phrase: "Faith without works is dead." James 2:14 asks, "What good is it . . . if someone says he has faith but does not have works?" And, of course, it's true! If our actions never prove our faith, is our faith really real? If I say I believe it's going to be a beautiful day today, but I pack my umbrella and galoshes, do I really believe it's going to be a beautiful day? Our actions really are the symptoms, the telltale signs, of our faith.

That being said, we live in a culture that places a high importance on making a way for yourself and being self-sustaining. In modern culture, it seems as though prayer is often viewed as the "lazy man's" answer, as if to say, "If you can't fix it yourself and you've already tried more practical options, try praying about it—it might just work." Of course, as believers we don't want to treat prayer this way, and I think we don't even realize when we *do* treat prayer this way. But our actions often tell a different story. In our relationships, in our jobs, with our finances, our gut reaction is often to work harder, communicate better, and find better resources, and prayer is often a last resort or an afterthought.

Let's say you and your partner are struggling with an issue. It could be that you feel they should change something they've been doing recently (or that they've always done). If they changed this habit, it would allow them to live more harmoniously with you, with others, and with God. You could confront them about the issue, ask them to change, and even bring in other godly people to counsel them into changing. As described in week 7 (page 19), all these actions could be great initiatives to take.

But what if you did something *before* taking those initiatives? What if, instead of leading with confrontation, you dealt with the issue by bringing it to God first? If God also feels the behavior needs to change, and if the timing is right, He will work in His own way to prepare your partner's heart for the coming change. Maybe, before you confront your partner about the issue, God has already quietly started to convince them of it Himself. By the time you sit down to talk with your partner, they might already be in sync with what you are feeling because God has already been working in their heart. If that's the case, your significant other will be much less likely to be defensive and much more likely to hear what you have to say because they realize God has been saying it to them all along.

Prayer *before* action is also a great way to make sure your own motives are in check. God might show you that the thing you want your partner to change is really just a personal preference rather than something ungodly. Say, for example, that it bothers you that your significant other seems to never pick up after themselves. Instead of confronting them about it right away as you might *like* to do, you take the time to pray over it and ask God if it's something you *should* do. During your time in prayer, God reveals to you that, although frustrating, your partner's tendency doesn't necessarily need to be confronted at this moment. Instead, God gives you more grace to overcome your frustration. Now, it may turn out that, later, God does confront their sloppiness, as it could reflect deeper issues of selfishness or laziness. But ultimately, the if and when of that confrontation is left up to God.

In your own relationship, do your best to make constant prayer a habit. When you sense feelings of frustration, pray. When you feel hurt, pray. And when things are going great, pray! Overall, God will help you have a healthy and godly view of the situation you're in and give you the wisdom to respond well, in a way that benefits both you and your significant other.

PRAYER

Ask God to remind you to bring all things to Him first before dealing with them on your own.

Pray that God would give you wisdom to discern when issues truly need confrontation and when they need grace.

Ask God to help you be patient in times of waiting for Him to act rather than acting yourself.

The Myth of the Soul Mate

Strive for peace with everyone, and for the holiness without which no one will see the Lord.

—

Hebrews 12:14

In week 32 (page 94), I talked about understanding personality types. What I mentioned but didn't emphasize is that after taking the Myers-Briggs Type Indicator personality assessment, Josh and I discovered just how different our personalities are. In fact, we looked up a chart that supposedly outlined which MBTI personalities were the most compatible, and Josh and I were on complete opposite ends of the chart—our personalities weren't considered just incompatible, but actually the *least* compatible with each other! We broke out laughing, not because we didn't believe it, but because we did! After being married for several years, it made complete sense to us that people would not recommend an extremely analytical personality to be matched up with an extremely emotional personality. So, seeing that chart, we had our laugh and then moved on with our day.

Other couples, whether married or in a dating relationship, might see this and begin to feel nervous. After all, our culture constantly feeds itself the romantic (yet terrifying) idea that everyone has a "soul mate" they are destined to find—or miss out on. Josh and I also struggled with this idea before we got married, although we

Christianized the term "soul mate" and called it "God's will" instead. We spent a lot of time worrying and praying that the person we were dating was the person God willed us to date. Something somewhere along the line had convinced us that God's will was like a path of destiny, and either you were on it or you weren't. Either you were making the choices God wanted you to make, or you weren't, and if you married the wrong person, you were outside of God's will.

It wasn't until we were married that God taught us a very simple but freeing truth (aren't so many of His truths like that?). And that truth is, *Every* relationship is made up of two very imperfect people, and *every* relationship takes work, sacrifice, and compromise. If you and your significant other love Jesus Christ and desire to obey His Word and live in a way that glorifies Him, your relationship will be pleasing to God. In general, God is not concerned with whom you enter into a relationship. He cares that both you and your significant other love Him more deeply than anything else in the world. If you can check that metaphorical box, then you might as well be checking "all of the above."

The reason I believe this is that in almost all references to marriage in the Bible, God is much more concerned with whether or not the relationship glorifies Him than with who specifically is in the relationship. He even addresses relationships between husbands and wives who are unequally yoked (i.e., one spouse is not a believer) and how they can live in a way that's pleasing to God to the best of their ability. There are a few circumstances in which God tells a man or woman to be in a relationship with someone He specifically chose (Mary and Joseph come to mind), but overall, He's less focused on *whom* we partner with than on *how* we relate to that person in a godly manner.

The concept of a soul mate might seem romantic, but in reality, it's a limiting notion that can make us miss out on meaningful relationships. If we allow ourselves to believe that the reason we're disagreeing or having a hard time with our significant other is because we're not "meant to be together," we miss out on countless opportunities to grow both personally and in our relationships. When relationships become hard, those who believe in soul mates can become convinced that they simply picked the wrong person and need to start over with someone else. Unfortunately, many married couples feel this way after years of marriage, which can lead to divorce. And many single people feel this way after a long string of dating relationships that never seem to work out.

Of course, not every dating relationship is meant to be permanent, but I've known too many couples who've spent countless days and nights trying to find some passage of Scripture or message from God to tell them whether their relationship is "God's will." If you're struggling with wondering whether or not you have found "the one," I hope this chapter encourages you. Seek God and love Him with your whole heart. Nothing else remotely compares to the peace and satisfaction you feel when you are content in Christ. Other things, including relationships, will fall into place.

PRAYER

Pray that you and your significant other would grow spiritually and find contentment and joy in Christ.

Ask that God would help you overcome conflicts and grow into a stronger, deeper relationship with your significant other.

Ask that all aspects of your life, including your relationship with your significant other, would bring glory to God.

Contentedness

Trust in the LORD, and do good; dwell in the land and befriend faithfulness. Delight yourself in the LORD, and he will give you the desires of your heart.

—

Psalm 37:3–4

It's funny how the things we want in life change over time. Like the material possessions we thought we couldn't live without or the job we pictured ourselves in. Even though we may look like adults on the outside, sometimes our need to immediately receive the things we want out of life proves that we have no more patience than children.

When I first started dating Josh, I knew he was the one I would marry—and I wanted to hurry up and do just that. (Of course, I was also pretty sure I was going to marry the couple of boyfriends that came before Josh.) You can imagine my impatience at having to date the man three years before we said, "I do." Once we finally said our vows, I had what I'd always wanted . . . and then reality set in.

Marriage wasn't as shiny and perfect as I had imagined it to be. Sure, I loved going to sleep and waking up next to my best friend every day, but we had a lot of kinks to sort out. There were many times early on in our marriage when both of us felt very alone, even though we had finally got the lifelong relationship we had wanted. It was then that we realized that the things people want out of life will always change. Once we do get the things we want, their shine almost immediately starts to dull, and we move on to the next thing we want.

It reminds me of the story of David and Bathsheba. King David decided that he wanted Bathsheba, even though she was already married to a soldier named Uriah. Instead of being content with what God had given him (like one of David's own wives, for instance), David took matters into his own hands and, well, got what he wanted. To hide the fact, he sent Uriah to the frontlines of the battlefield, where he was killed in combat. David didn't realize the consequences of taking whatever he wanted until it was too late and he had already "displeased the LORD" (2 Samuel 11:27). If he had been content with what God had already given him, he wouldn't have had to suffer the pain of taking matters into his own hands and turning a blind eye to what God clearly wanted.

The truth of the matter is, when we fight for the things that we want, even when we can feel God whispering to us to wait, we are choosing to make those things idols. It shows that we're discontent with where God has placed us in the now and that we're not using our current state to bring glory to God. Of course, this doesn't have to take place only in relationships. As I said earlier, we could be unsatisfied with our jobs, our homes, our families, even our church.

In what areas of your life might you be feeling discontent right now? In what ways could you be active and working toward bringing glory to God in your time of waiting? If there are things in your life that you have been impatiently waiting for, I encourage you to surrender them to God. Ultimately, apart from Christ, those things will not give you the feeling you're looking for, whether that's security, happiness, success, recognition, or anything else. While none of those things is inherently bad, ask yourself the honest question, "Would I still be content in Christ even if I didn't have these things?"

PRAYER

Ask God to help you identify areas of impatience in your life.

Ask God to reveal ways you can use your time of waiting to glorify Him and serve others.

Ask God what He would like to teach you during your time of waiting.

Don't Let It Go

Preach the word; be ready in season and out of season; reprove,
rebuke, and exhort, with complete patience and teaching.
—

2 Timothy 4:2

As I mentioned earlier, when Josh and I first started dating, my skill level at confrontation was somewhere near zero. Josh, on the other hand, was great at confrontation! So whenever a disagreement came up, guess which one of us did the most talking? Josh. By far.

At the time, I figured that I was doing the selfless thing by holding my tongue, "forgiving" him, and not starting a fight about something he had done that hurt my feelings. Instead, I shoved my feelings under the rug until enough time passed that whatever he did stopped bothering me, at least for a while. Then, after the same thing that had hurt me the first time happened a few more times, there finally came the last straw. I would break down and cry or become extremely angry, which was pretty out of character for me. I just couldn't believe how he could continue to hurt me!

What I didn't realize at the time was this: I never told Josh that he had hurt me, so he never realized he had hurt me, so ... he kept on hurting me. When he continued to hurt my feelings, it was partially my fault. I could have talked to him about it the very first time it happened, or any of the times after, but instead, I decided it would be better to "not get into it" or "let it go." And because of this, I ended up thinking my boyfriend was heartless, while Josh ended up blindsided when I couldn't take it anymore.

Eventually, I learned that the sooner I brought up something that bothered me, in a loving and nonjudgmental way, the sooner Josh and I could start working on it. Sometimes it's okay to let go of things that bother me, as we're both imperfect and need a little unspoken forgiveness from time to time, but if I actually want an action of his to change in the long run, I need to be transparent with him.

To do that, first, I try my best to make sure that *my will* aligns with *God's will*. Okay, maybe the fact that Josh left his laundry on the floor isn't really addressed in the Bible, but, within reason, Josh could serve me and love me, as God calls couples to do, and that might involve remembering to put his laundry in the hamper. Additionally, I try to determine whether his actions are just a quirk I should try to get used to or if they're something I could justify asking him to change. Over time, it has become easier to decide when to confront him about something and when to let it go.

You will find your own balance within your relationship. There will, of course, be times when it's the best thing for your relationship to just let it go. But there will be other times when you'll need to have those uncomfortable or difficult conversations. When you do, do your best to explain or even overexplain your feelings, why you think it's important to have the conversation, and how you hope it will help your relationship in the long run. It's also extremely useful to reiterate how much you love and respect your partner. Affirmation can go a long way in moments of confrontation.

At the end of the day, be sure to cover all of your confrontations, your hurt feelings, and your relationship in general in prayer. Don't underestimate the work that God can do in your significant other's heart as well as yours when it comes to hurt and restoration.

PRAYER

Pray that God would prepare both your heart and your significant other's heart for confrontation.

Ask that God would give you the boldness to bring up small hurts before they fester into large wounds.

Ask God for the wisdom to bring things up in a way that is helpful, honest, and appropriate for your relationship with each other and your relationships with Him.

Set an Example

But I received mercy for this reason, that in me, as the foremost, Jesus Christ might display his perfect patience as an example to those who were to believe in him for eternal life.

—

1 Timothy 1:16

The closer you become with someone, the easier it is to become frustrated with them. When you and your significant other first started dating, you were probably very quick to forgive them if they forgot a special day, said something that may have rubbed you the wrong way, or did something seemingly selfish like eat the last bit of ice cream.

But when you begin to deepen the relationship, your standards for your partner may begin to shift. Suddenly, their eating the last bit of ice cream may not seem so cute. It may be harder to be understanding if they forget to pick you up after work. Essentially, the more you get to know your significant other, the more you'll become familiar with their failings.

As we've discussed, having open communication and developing your skills at confrontation are extremely important. If you go your entire relationship simply absorbing the hurt that you feel when your significant other lets you down, there isn't much sense in having hope that your relationship will improve. And, like a sponge, eventually that hurt will seep out.

That being said, sometimes you will just have to absorb the hurt. There may come a day when you lose count of the times you asked your significant other to change a behavior. They're at a point where they very clearly understand how you feel, but change is not on the horizon. It's important to note here that just because you have invested a certain amount of time in a relationship, it never means you have to *remain* in the relationship if you feel as though the area where you're asking for change is a "deal breaker." (Of course, I'm talking about dating relationships here). But there may come a time in your relationship when, even though you aren't seeing the change you would like to see, the better choice is still to stay.

In Philippians 3:12, Paul talks about the work God has done in him and is continuously doing in him: "Not that I have already obtained this or am already perfect, but I press on to make it my own, because Christ Jesus has made me his own." He goes on to admit that he isn't perfect, but he strives to improve himself and follow the example that Christ sets. He ends the passage by saying, "Let those of us who are mature think this way, and if in anything you think otherwise, God will reveal that also to you. Only let us hold true to what we have attained" (Phillipians 3:15–16).

Paul understands that not every believer will have the same spiritual maturity as every other believer. He knows what *he* has learned so far from God's Word, but he knows that not everyone may have learned yet what he has learned. Even so, he's not going to compromise what he has already learned, but he *will* be patient with those who may not be as far along in their walk with Christ.

This same scenario may be true in your own relationship. You may have a more mature spiritual understanding than your significant other in certain areas. If that's the case, it's important to stand on what you know to be true, but it's also important to be patient with those who are still learning. Paul understands that he may be more spiritually mature in certain areas than others, and he also admits that he, too, is still learning and therefore needs to keep a humble attitude.

So how can we apply this when we ask our significant other for change and then fail to see it happen? We can take the opportunity to set an example, rather than trying to force change. Along with this, we can pray for our partner's growth and that, if it would be God's will, that they would seek to change on their own. You may be surprised by what God decides to teach them in His own timing. Until then, do your best to stick to what God has taught *you* and live it out as an example to your significant other.

PRAYER

When you would like to see change in your significant other, go to God about it first. Ask Him if the change you would like to see is His will or simply your own.

Ask that God would give you the strength and spiritual maturity to stick to the things He has revealed to you so far in your relationship with Him.

Continuously pray that God work in the life of your significant other and continue to grow them spiritually.

Let the Past Pass

For I am the least of the apostles, unworthy to be called an apostle, because I persecuted the church of God. But by the grace of God I am what I am, and his grace toward me was not in vain. On the contrary, I worked harder than any of them, though it was not I, but the grace of God that is with me.

—

1 Corinthians 15:9–10

Many of us have entered into relationships when the wounds from our previous relationship were still healing. You may struggle to trust someone new after the last person you dated lied or otherwise hurt you, or you might be scared you'll make the same mistakes as last time. You might even wonder if you'll ever find love and get married. Because of all that, you may find yourself having a hard time opening up and being vulnerable with someone new.

While I wouldn't say I had trouble trusting again (at 18, I probably could have used a little *more* distrust), it was difficult for me to open up about my past relationships to Josh. I had treated those previous boyfriends as idols, holding so tight to them that I often pushed God to the back burner. Did it backfire? You betcha. But in high school, that pattern seemed perpetual. It wasn't until later that I learned that only a love for Christ can create the type of relationship I was dreaming of.

Josh had also dated a few girls before we met, and in the early days of our relationship, I felt a twinge of pain when thinking of him having feelings for someone else, even though I had also dated in the past. I worried that I was inferior to his past girlfriends in some way or that he might somehow wish he were back together with one of them instead of with me.

How can we move on from past relationships and past hurts into new relationships that are healthy, functional, and glorifying to God?

I'll share something I learned that changed my relationship with Josh (and every other relationship in my life). For years, I'd been focused on being "good enough" for God. I also wanted to be a good enough girlfriend. In my relationships, both with God and with men, I had always made huge efforts to try to "read" how they felt about me on a day-to-day or even hour-to-hour basis. Josh struggled with this, too, also worrying about whether he was truly accepted by God. But Luke 10:27 tells us, "You shall love the Lord your God with all your heart and with all your soul and with all your strength and with all your mind, and your neighbor as yourself." It wasn't until we realized that it wasn't about *what we did* but about *who we loved* that everything changed.

First, we had to find our security in Christ rather than in each other, which was something we had both been struggling with. Once we realized that all Christ truly wants from us is to love and enjoy Him more than anything else in the world, our worries about whether or not we were good enough began to fade away. We were too busy enjoying Christ to worry about whether our place in heaven was secure, and that was actually all Jesus wanted from us anyway. Once this happened, our grip on our relationship with each other began to loosen and we started to hold our relationship with an open hand, ready for Christ to do what He wanted with it.

Our focus slowly began to shift from our past mistakes to how we could reach others and share with them the joy and freedom we found in Christ. Instead of letting those mistakes tear us down, we thought of ways we could use them to relate to and help others. There was a time when I wished I could just delete my previous relationships so my relationship with Josh would be my first and only one. But after realizing I can put my past pain to current use, I no longer want to blot out my past. Instead, I use the lessons I learned to relate to the people around me and speak experienced truth into their lives.

I want to encourage you and your significant other to run toward Christ with everything you've got. He makes all things new and is able to use your past hurts in ways you may not have imagined. If you and your significant other are both running full force toward Christ and holding your relationship in an open hand, ready for God to use it, trusting your significant other becomes far less of an issue. Yes, there may still be pain to work through. There may still be hard conversations to have. But there's something about being in a relationship with someone who knows they have been saved by grace: Those who know they have been given grace are far more likely to extend that same grace to others.

That being the case, when you're in a dating relationship, guard your heart but pray about being open with your partner. Over time, as you build trust, allow God to heal your past wounds and work toward an open and trusting relationship with your significant other.

PRAYER

Ask that God would allow your past wounds to heal and help you give those past hurts over to Him.

Ask that God would use your past to reach others for His glory.

Ask that God would allow you to build a grace-filled and trusting relationship with your partner.

Fill Your Mind with God

If then you have been raised with Christ, seek the things that are above, where Christ is, seated at the right hand of God. Set your minds on things that are above, not on things that are on earth. For you have died, and your life is hidden with Christ in God.

—

Colossians 3:1–3

How do you usually spend your free time or idle moments? Which accounts do you follow on social media? What TV shows do you sit and watch at the end of the day?

A few years ago, Josh and I decided to try watching *The Walking Dead,* a show set in a future America overrun by zombies. At first, I'd keep my eyes covered for at least half of each episode, trying to avoid the gruesomeness. But the more we watched, the less I covered my eyes. I started to get used to the gory scenes and eventually didn't mind them so much. During the day, while at work or in class, my mind drifted to the show and its storyline, wondering what would happen next and how the characters would react. If I ran an errand at night and returned home when it was dark, my eyes would involuntarily glance over at the shadowy woods as I was walking from the car to the house. Of course, I knew there were no zombies in the woods. Probably.

Also around this time, I began to have nightmares. I didn't realize just how much of my mind the show was starting to consume, and how desensitized I'd become to scenes of violence and pain. In between *Walking Dead* seasons, when our TV fare consisted of much more pleasant shows, there was a large cluster of acts of violence and terror taking place both in the United States and overseas. My heart went out to the people affected by those attacks, and I couldn't help but wonder: If I were in the middle of a *Walking Dead* binge and accustomed to seeing daily scenes of gruesome pain, would I be able to have as much empathy for those people? Or would I be numb to their plight, shutting it out as just another example of horror playing out on my TV screen? I wanted to have empathy when it came to other people's pain. I *wanted* it to bother me.

When the next season of *The Walking Dead* was available to watch, Josh asked me if I wanted to start it up again. I replied, "Honestly, no." And he agreed.

I share this story to illustrate how what we put into our minds affects how we relate to the world. If you have a job with coworkers who talk a lot about material possessions, after a while, you'll start to think materialistically, too. If you hang out with people who make degrading sexual comments about women, you'll start to think that way, too. What you allow to be put into your mind eventually starts to make its way out into your words.

Of course, we can't live effectively as Christians if we decide to exist in a bubble, separate from the rest of the world. Not every believer has the ability to work in a Christian workplace, nor should we! But if we can't fully separate ourselves from worldly things, how do we keep them from infiltrating our minds and overflowing into the rest of our lives?

The key is to constantly be filling our minds with the things of God. In this way, we can live alongside the rest of the world, alongside nonbelievers, and still be filled with God's truth. If we spend time daily in God's Word and in communication with Him, He will enable us to live a life that glorifies Him, even among those who do not believe. And, as we do so, nonbelievers will see how Christ makes us want to live differently from the rest of the world.

Focusing our attention on godly things will also make us better able to discern God's truth in a world where we are constantly fed alternate versions of the truth. In a world that undermines the value of life, you will know that God's truth says, "God created man in his own image" (Genesis 1:27). In a world that tells you to love yourself, you will know that God's Word says, "You shall love the Lord your God with all your heart and with all your soul and with all your mind. This is the great and first commandment" (Matthew 22:37–38).

In your daily life, join your significant other in seeking to fill your mind with the things of Christ. That way, you'll be able to live in the world while still maintaining a mind-set and lifestyle that is set apart from the world.

PRAYER

Ask that God would enable you to discern the difference between His truth and the world's truth.

Ask God to give you empathy for those around you.

Ask God to help you keep your mind on things that are from Him and His Word instead of things that are of the world.

The Limits of Happiness

Do nothing from rivalry or conceit, but in humility count others more significant than yourselves.

—

Philippians 2:3

I've seen many people enter into a string of relationships, experiencing one breakup after another. So much of their time is wasted dating people who they thought would make *them* happy and then becoming disappointed. I've even seen marriages end because one or both spouses said their spouse no longer made them happy. What's sad is that these couples are missing one of the most basic but important truths about godly relationships: Marriage, and the relationships that lead up to it, were not created simply to make *individuals* happy.

The purpose of marriage is to be a picture of Christ's relationship to the church, and to have a strong and godly foundation on which to build a family. In the Garden of Eden, God did not say he gave Adam a spouse only to make him *happy*. And while Scripture points out that romantic relationships, specifically marriage, can be very joyful ("Let your fountain be blessed, and rejoice in the wife of your youth," Proverbs 5:18), nowhere does it lead us to believe that relationships simply serve the purpose of making us content. Marriage may help us refrain from sexual immorality, it can give us a way to collaborate with our spiritual gifts, and it can be a medium through which we portray the Gospel. But if we seek out romantic relationships, and ultimately marriage, simply for our own benefit, we miss out on its greatest purpose.

In looking at marriage (and dating relationships) as a reflection of Christ's relationship with the church, we find a wonderful opportunity to love and serve an individual in a way that no other person can. Peter wrote this to wives with unsaved husbands, but I think it applies to all believers: "Likewise, wives, be subject to your own husbands, so that even if some do not obey the word, they may be won without a word by the conduct of their wives, when they see your respectful and pure conduct" (1 Peter 3:1–2). Who has a better opportunity than you to pray for, serve, and love your significant other? Who can better set a godly example for them, edify them, and encourage them on their walk with the Lord? Of course, there may/should be pastors or other spiritual leaders who your significant other looks up to, but you have the opportunity to know the intricacies of their life and speak Gospel truths to them, by word or deed, on a daily basis. How cool is that?

When we spend our time focusing on how we can encourage and support our significant other (not to mention make *them* happy), we start to worry less about whether we ourselves are happy enough. In *The Purpose Driven Life*, Rick Warren says, "Humility is not thinking less of yourself, it's thinking of yourself less." I've seen so many relationships split in two because one or both parties were unable to work through their naturally occurring entitlement and selfishness. I've also seen many individuals sadly say something along the lines of, "God wants me to be happy." This is a sad thought because simply being happy, apart from God, is a temporary lie. God wants us to find joy *in Him*, not just to *be happy*. Happiness is a temporary feeling. The joy that God gives is eternal and real.

If we spend our time thinking about whether or not our significant other is making *us* happy enough, we lose out on so many opportunities to show them true love by loving them even when it doesn't come naturally or easily. But if you deprioritize your own happiness, you can set the standard in your relationship of self-sacrificial love that both pleases God and edifies your significant other. In doing so, you become like Christ to your significant other, which, after all, is the purpose of marriage, isn't it? And dating relationships are practice for that life-long relationship.

Of course, only God enables us to love in this way. We cannot, of our own power, self-sacrificially love our significant other. Any godly and faithful act we do comes straight from the Holy Spirit Himself, who lives inside us.

PRAYER

Ask that God would enable you to think of others as more important than yourself.

Ask God to help you identify ways in which you can serve and love your significant other, especially when it doesn't come naturally.

Ask God to prepare you to be the type of person who can set a godly example for your future spouse.

Use Your Time Together Wisely

And whatever you do, in word or deed, do everything in the name of the Lord Jesus, giving thanks to God the Father through him.
—

Colossians 3:17

In week 3 (page 7), I talked about prioritizing your time with your significant other. This week, I want to talk about using that time wisely and getting the most out of it. In that chapter, I talked about couples who fall into something more like a collaborative partnership than a loving and intimate relationship. Sure, that kind of setup may work like a well-oiled machine, but it's probably not the relationship you dreamed of having, or even the relationship that God would desire you to have with your future spouse (after all, Christ's relationship with His bride isn't simply functional, it's an intimate and enjoyable relationship).

The longer you and your significant other are in a relationship together, the more you will begin to "settle in." As you're living life together, you may find yourselves in an unintentional routine. At 5 p.m. you return home from your day, by 6 you're eating dinner, and then it's on to your latest Netflix binge. Of course, everyone needs time to decompress from work, school, ministry, and so on, and yeah, TV or social media might be a part of that. But I also want to encourage both you and your significant other to make a habit of finding productive ways of making your free time together *quality* time in every sense of the word.

As mentioned in week 3 (page 7), it's important to carve out time in your schedule specifically for each other and to have one really good conversation each day. But there are other ways you can make the most of your time together, as well. Serving in ministry is a great one, of course, but so are developing new hobbies together, working toward health and fitness goals together, or even finding ways to start a small business together. However you decide to spend real quality time with your significant other, find things that will help you grow in your relationship with each other, grow closer to God, help others, and/or be productive in some way. It will allow you to get to know each other in ways that go beyond questions and answers or conversation. You'll be able to observe how your significant other handles complicated situations and new ideas, and how you both work together as a team.

In my own relationship, I didn't realize how compassionate a person Josh was until he and I were serving in ministry together. More than once, I saw him go out of his way to go back and deliver lunch to a homeless person he had seen on the side of the road. I never would have seen this side of him if most of our quality time had been spent sitting and simply talking or scrolling through our phones together. Sure, he could have told me about that time he got lunch for a homeless person, but I wouldn't have seen firsthand the compassion he showed had we not been using our free time in that way.

Whether it's feeding the homeless or something else entirely, there are any number of ways you can use your time together with your significant other. Do something with a purpose you can both be proud of.

PRAYER

Ask God to show you ways that you can use your time as a couple more productively.

Ask God to give you wisdom to discern between being overly involved in extra activities and using your time in productive ways.

Ask God to allow you and your significant other to work well as a team and make the most of your time together.

Working Through Anger

Be angry and do not sin; do not let the sun go down on your anger.
—

Ephesians 4:26

Anger can take many forms. It can be loud and aggressive, or quiet and bitter. It can be righteous, vengeful, spiteful, or jealous. It can rise and fall in an instant, or burn slowly for years.

We can learn from reading God's Word that anger itself is not sinful. Many times in the Old Testament we hear of God's anger toward the Israelites or another group of people. For example: "And the Lord's anger was kindled against Israel, and He made them wander in the wilderness forty years" (Numbers 32:13). In the New Testament, we hear of Jesus's anger when the money changers and those who sold animals for sacrifices set themselves up in the temple. Anger is a natural reaction to a situation in which things are not the way we feel they should be. It's our emotional response when we or someone we love is mistreated. Of course, God's anger is always righteous, whereas often ours is . . . not. So how can we learn from His righteous anger to transform the anger we feel from time to time?

First, remember that the thing that makes you angry should be directly compared with God's Word. Ask yourself, "Why am I feeling angry right now? What thing that I love is being wronged or mistreated and causing me to feel angry?" Maybe you feel angry because no one seems to recognize or appreciate the hard work you do on a regular basis. In that instance, what is the thing you love and want to protect? Yourself. And more often than not, we'll find that the reason for our anger stems from our own pride and selfishness rather than a love for God. In moments like these, we can use our anger to ask ourselves what we truly love. If we find that it's ourselves, we can use that instance of anger as an impetus for self-reflection and repentance, asking Christ to remove our pride and replace it with His holiness.

Here's an example: I ask Josh to pick me up from the store at 3 p.m. When he doesn't arrive until 3:20, I'm pretty mad. He may or may not have a good reason for being late. It could be traffic, or maybe he misplaced his keys. I don't really have anywhere to be after shopping, but I'm still mad that I had to wait 20 minutes longer than I intended. In this scenario, what is the thing I'm loving? If I'm being completely honest, I'm loving myself. It's my pride that tells me I shouldn't have had to wait 20 minutes when I asked Josh to be there at a certain time. It's my pride that tells me being inconvenienced is not okay.

Galatians 2:20 says, "I have been crucified with Christ. It is no longer I who live, but Christ who lives in me. And the life I now live in the flesh I live by faith in the Son of God, who loved me and gave himself for me." If we live by that verse, being inconvenienced or mistreated no longer creates feelings of spite, because we don't have the ego to insist our needs come first.

Of course, as Jesus showed us, there are instances when anger is righteous. In those instances, the thing being mistreated or misrepresented is God or the things of God, as when Jesus became angry with the money changers because they were detracting from God being made great in His temple. There may be times when we become angry in defense of someone else, and while this anger may be justified, it's important to remember Ephesians 4:26: "Be angry and do not sin." Ask God for wisdom and do your best to determine whether or not it would be better to turn the other cheek and let God handle the situation, or to work toward correcting the injustice. Even if your anger makes perfect sense, remember what Romans 12:19 says, "Beloved, never avenge yourselves, but leave it to the wrath of God, for it is written, 'Vengeance is mine, I will repay, says the Lord.'"

When you have anger toward your significant other (and from time to time you very likely will), it's important, just as in any Christian relationship, to eventually reconcile and find unity in Christ. Things like communication, confrontation, repentance, and forgiveness are also relevant here, but in the end, we are told "If possible, so far as it depends on you, live peaceably with all" (Romans 12:18). In your relationship, always try to take steps to work toward that together.

There are times when serious tendencies toward anger may need the help of a professional. If severe outbreaks of anger are something you struggle with, protect both yourself and your significant other by seeking a godly individual who is able to pray and counsel you through those feelings and teach you healthy ways to manage them.

PRAYER

Ask that God would daily allow you to die to yourself and live by faith in Him.

When you begin to feel angry, ask God to remind you to consider others as more significant than yourself.

In situations when your significant other may be angry, pray for God to work in their heart and subdue those feelings so you and your partner can communicate more effectively.

Accepting Christ's Forgiveness

For while we were still weak, at the right time Christ died for the ungodly. For one will scarcely die for a righteous person—though perhaps for a good person one would dare even to die—but God shows his love for us in that while we were still sinners, Christ died for us.

—

Romans 5:6–8

Have you ever let someone down and then felt incredibly ashamed about it? Maybe this wasn't the first time you let this person down, so your apologies and promises to do better next time have lost their meaning. You can feel their disappointment.

When I was pretty young, I used to have what I would say was an unhealthy fear of God. I used to picture a big old man looking down on me with a frown and shaking his head in disappointment. If I spent several days in a row reading my Bible, or if I did something for someone in need, I felt like God and I were pretty good, and that He was happy with me for a while. But eventually I would see that frowning old man looking down on me again, disappointed in what I had just done.

When I got older, I began to grow tired of envisioning God constantly disappointed in me and shaking his head, so I preferred not to think of Him at all. I decided that I was going to live my life how I felt like it and push God as far to the back of my mind as I could, and I would be happier that way. It didn't take very long for me to realize that something was missing. Life felt emptier when I was living for myself. Eventually, I began to let Him into my life again. But I still couldn't shake the feeling that He was disappointed in me. I wanted more than anything to prove myself to God but, inevitably, I would fail Him.

One day, in college, I was spending alone time with God and reading a passage of Scripture, and all of a sudden, it was as if God directly said, "Stop trying to prove your worth to Me. You're already Mine, and nothing will change that. Start enjoying Me."

And it finally made sense. I had been struggling to organize my priorities so that God always came first. The problem was, I was always so scared that I wasn't doing enough or living well enough. My fear kept me from truly enjoying who God was. What I didn't realize was that if I truly and simply found joy in Christ, everything else would fall into place. I might make mistakes here and there, but Jesus promises to forgive us and complete what he started in us.

In his letter to the Philippians, Paul deliberates about whether he would rather die and be with God in heaven or stay on earth and continue furthering the Gospel. He writes, "Convinced of this, I know that I will remain and continue with you all, for your progress and joy in the faith" (Philippians 1:25). Finding joy in Christ is one of the most essential things we can do as Christians. If we hold on too tightly to our past sins and guilt, we keep ourselves from truly experiencing the joy we can have in knowing Christ. If we constantly picture God's disappointment and consider ourselves unworthy, we withhold ourselves from living the freedom of His forgiveness! To paraphrase Romans 8:17, if, once forgiven, we are considered to be God's heirs with Christ, how much freedom and forgiveness and love and acceptance does that mean we have in God's presence?

I want to encourage you, if you struggle with holding on to your guilt and shame but know that you have been forgiven by Christ, to live joyfully in Him! Pursue a relationship with Him with all your heart! You can be sure that He is also pursuing you. Turn over your guilt and shame to Him and finally find rest in the peace He provides you.

PRAYER

Ask that God would reveal to you what it means to truly find joy in Him.

Ask God to allow you to shed the burdens of guilt and shame at the cross and take on your new life as a co-heir with Christ.

Pray that your significant other would pursue Christ with their whole heart and live joyfully knowing Him.

Learn to Be Flexible

Let not the one who eats despise the one who abstains, and let not the one who abstains pass judgment on the one who eats, for God has welcomed him. Who are you to pass judgment on the servant of another?
—

Romans 14:3–4

When you enter into a committed relationship with someone, you will most likely have to adapt to each other's habits and customs. Those habits and customs are most often inherited from your family. What if your family has always done something a certain way and your significant other's family does it a different way? Are you going to insist that the way you were raised is the right way, or, on the other end of the spectrum, will you be so infatuated with your partner that you'll forget about your traditions and adopt all the ways they do things? As this week's Bible verse shows, there are ways to nonjudgmentally accommodate each other.

Let's consider a simple family dinner. Say your family made sit-down dinners a priority every night, whereas in your partner's family, each person usually ate whenever it was convenient for them and their schedule. How will you compromise about that when sharing meals with your partner starts to become a big part of your life? In my family, we sat down to eat together, and Josh's family's tendency to eat separately was completely foreign to me at first. I was sure my way was better—but over time, I noticed that my family didn't do as great a job of spending time together away from the dinner table, whereas Josh's family would often come together and hang out or watch a movie together in the evening when everyone was finally home. My notion that everyone had to be at the dinner table at the same time every day slowly disappeared as I realized that as long as family time is a priority, it doesn't matter whether it happens over dinner or sitting together in the living room later in the evening. Both approaches are valid.

Before any of these issues creates ill feelings between you and your significant other, either toward each other or toward your families, it's important to realize that simply because you grew up doing things one way, that doesn't mean it's the *only* way or even necessarily a *good* way. Both of you should be prepared to take a step back and think critically about why you do the things you do and how important it really is to keep doing things that way.

In your relationship, make a point to occasionally step outside your own habits, customs, and routines to see where the two of you can become more flexible. When you find something that you've both done significantly differently for a long time, do your best to find a middle ground that won't have either of you arguing over who does it "better." This communication will be especially important when you and your significant other start spending time with each other's families, who may question why you've changed what you do or why your partner does things a certain way. If you're at an appropriate stage in the "leaving and cleaving" process described in week 2 (page 4), be ready to support your partner and show your family that you and your partner are united.

The book of Acts includes a description of many new and different believers coming together to join the early church and live a new life: "Parthians and Medes and Elamites and residents of Mesopotamia, Judea and Cappadocia, Pontus and Asia, Phrygia and Pamphylia, Egypt and the parts of Libya belonging to Cyrene, and visitors from Rome, both Jews and proselytes, Cretans and Arabians" (Acts 2:9–11). What better way for you and your significant other to carry on that example than by being flexible and open with each other's backgrounds? Even if you find it hard to adapt to something, like what they do for fun, how they communicate, or how they eat dinner, having an open mind and loving them with an outpouring of Christ's love will be the best way you can glorify God.

And who knows? Eventually, you may even grow to like the way your significant other and their family do things. You'll have two backgrounds to draw from when you start to create your own traditions together.

PRAYER

Ask God to help you judge all things against His Word, be flexible, and have an open mind.

Ask God to give you extra grace to overcome social or cultural boundaries between your significant other and yourself.

Leadership in the Dating Relationship

Wives, submit to your own husbands, as to the Lord. . . . Husbands, love your wives, as Christ loved the church and gave himself up for her.

—

Ephesians 5:22, 25

I'm sure you've heard this before: In a biblical marriage, God calls each partner to specific roles within that relationship. He calls men to lead and women to support. (I'll dive into what exactly that looks like in a minute.) But what about in a dating relationship? How does this principle apply if you're not actually married?

First, let's break down what exactly the Bible means when it talks about headship and submission. In a marriage, God calls the man to be the head. In doing this, he expects the husband to be the provider and spiritual leader of the family. As a complementary role, God calls the woman to support, and in the process, respect her husband.

It's been a long time since the Bible was written, and in our culture, it's easy for women to become offended by the fact that they were not asked by God to have equal leadership roles in the relationship. However, this thinking assumes that God does not consider women as competent as men.

What we need to understand about leadership is that it is much more about *initiative* than it is about *competency*. A person who is in leadership will not necessarily be the best at all things. For example, I'm much better at keeping track of our finances than Josh is. However, as the leader of our relationship, he takes the initiative to ask me to make a budget, because he know's that it's something I have a better understanding of.

Another thing we need to consider is that submission does not mean *unquestioning* submission. When making a decision as a couple, both parties are involved and aware of all aspects of the decision. The husband may ask his wife what she thinks would be the best option, and she will have her own unique insights to share. However, the husband will ultimately make the final decision, and the wife will trust her husband because she understands that he is ultimately responsible to God for leading his home to the best of his ability.

How can we apply this to the dating relationship, when a couple is not yet living under the oath of marriage?

You may not be fully disclosing your financial decisions to each other, and in many ways you will still be independent of each other, but dating should often be looked at as a trial for marriage. Guys, how often do you initiate making decisions? Ladies, how likely are you to follow your boyfriend's lead?

Of course, both these roles become much easier to follow and align ourselves with when we know that our significant other is pursuing the will of God, just like we are. If, as women, we know that our boyfriend pursues Christ, knowing Him, desiring to honor Him, and submitting to Him, then following his lead becomes much easier. If we, as women, ultimately submit ourselves to God, it's natural to submit to someone in leadership who is also submitting themselves to God. For men, it becomes much easier to lead when your girlfriend desires to help and support in any way possible because you both have the common goal of honoring God with your lives.

As you grow together in your relationship and move closer to the possibility of marriage, your complementary roles should look more and more like a biblical marriage. However, this type of leadership and submission cannot, and should not, come before knowing the other person's heart. It takes time and trust to develop—which doesn't necessarily mean you should date for five years before you get married, but it does mean you should work toward getting to know each other on a deeper level, growing spiritually, and openly sharing what God is doing in your lives. Of course, this isn't done with the intent to prove your spirituality to each other. It will happen naturally when you and your partner "love the Lord your God with all your heart and with all your soul and with all your strength and with all your mind" (Luke 10:27).

In your dating relationship, understand that God made both male and female with equal competencies, calling men to initiate and women to support. Ultimately, both men and women submit themselves to Christ. Both roles are self-sacrificial. Both overflow with the love of Christ, and both treat the other as more significant than themselves.

PRAYER

Pray that God would help you have a clear understanding of biblical headship and submission.

Ask that God would help you and your significant other have an appropriate level of leadership and submission in your dating relationship.

Thank God for providing an example in His Word, through Christ's relationship with the church, of what biblical leadership and submission look like.

Money Matters

Wealth gained hastily will dwindle, but whoever gathers little by little will increase it.

—

Proverbs 13:11

Back in week 6 (page 16), we talked about the love of money (or the things money can buy), and how it can come between you and God. We also talked about how looking at bank statements can help you see where your priorities really lie. This week, I want to talk about budgeting and financial planning. Once you've looked at where your money goes, how do you and your significant other bring your spending into better alignment with God's will, both individually and as a couple?

Money is often seen as a private topic, and many couples are unaware of each other's spending and saving habits before they get married. You might be aware that your significant other has student-loan debt, and you may agree that purchasing a home is on the list of long-term goals for both of you. But have you talked about the time frame in which you'll want to pay off those loans? Or the things you may need to cut out of your budget in order to afford a house?

My mom likes to tell a story about how she and my dad were not always wise with their money. In the beginning of their marriage, they had several credit cards and took out loans in order to pay for a new house. Over time, their debt grew, and as they were both living on teacher's salaries, they struggled to pay it off. She says that at one point, they ate hot dogs for dinner every night for an entire summer.

I remember when they started going to church in the evenings with several other couples to do Dave Ramsey's Financial Peace University program. My mom put money in envelopes labeled Groceries, Utilities, Clothes, and so on. I remember those envelopes going everywhere she did, and I remember her getting a pair of scissors and cutting up several credit cards at the kitchen table.

While my mom and dad didn't start their marriage in an ideal place financially, they were able to evaluate their habits and realize that if they kept doing what they were used to doing, they would find themselves in trouble. They first decided to take an honest look at their finances. Then, when they saw that more money was going out than was coming in, they made difficult choices about where to cut excess spending and worked hard at paying off their debt more intentionally than they had in the past. Through all this, they sought advice from those who had gone before them and knew more than they did about the world of finances. I'm thankful for the example of humility and self-sacrifice they set for me and my siblings.

In your own relationship, take the time to learn from others who know more than you and have more experience with financial planning. Listen to Dave Ramsey's radio show (www.DaveDamsey.com/Show) and/or podcast (www.DaveRamsey.com/Show/Podcasts) together in the car in order to learn healthy budgeting and spending habits. As your relationship grows and as you feel more comfortable with it, start having more conversations about money—how you'd like to save it, and how you can plan to spend it wisely. By the time you and your significant other get married, finances should be something that you can speak openly and often about. When you pray together, try to remember to ask God to give you wisdom when it comes to finances— to know when to be frugal, when to be generous, and when it's okay to purchase something that would simply be nice to have. Make planning out your own personal budgets into a fun activity that you can do side by side while you're dating and as a unit when you're married.

PRAYER

Ask God to help you and your significant other hold your spending habits with an open hand.

Ask that God would give you wisdom when deciding when to spend, when to save, and when to be generous.

Ask God to bless your efforts in being intentional and wise with your money.

Keeping Your Lamp Lit

And all who believed were together and had all things in common. And they were selling their possessions and belongings and distributing the proceeds to all, as any had need. And day by day, attending the temple together and breaking bread in their homes, they received their food with glad and generous hearts.

—

Acts 2:44–46

Before Josh and I moved to the other side of the country, we were part of a community group that we loved deeply. A major theme in our group was learning how to live in Christian community with each other. We talked about the challenges we face when it comes to living in community with other believers, things like encouraging each other when needed, serving each other, and praying for each other. Why don't we do these things more often? Why don't they come to us more naturally?

I believe there are two underlying reasons why Christians can find it challenging to move in godly community with each other. The first is a lack of empathy. To put it bluntly, the struggles that our brothers and sisters in Christ go through often don't mean enough to us that we stop what we're doing and jump in to help wherever needed. I'm guilty of this as well—how often have I simply listened and nodded without offering help when a friend expressed their struggles to me? If I truly cared deeply that my friend was struggling to complete her to-do list, wouldn't I make more of an effort to help her accomplish those goals rather than simply listen to her express her troubles?

The second reason we sometimes don't engage in real Christian community is that, although we care and have a desire to help, our schedules and responsibilities often get in the way. But what if we arranged our schedules in such a way that we always had the time and resources to help fellow believers when needed?

Think of Jesus's parable of the ten virgins, who were all part of a wedding ceremony. "Five were wise" and brought extra oil to keep their lamps lit while waiting for the groom to arrive, but "five of them were foolish" and did not (Matthew 25:2). The groom got held up, and as the night wore on, the ten women fell asleep, and their lamps eventually burned out. When, at midnight, the groom finally did arrive, the five foolish virgins had no oil to relight their lamps. They had to run out and try to buy some at the last minute, and they ended up missing the wedding. But the women who had planned ahead had enough oil at the time the bridegroom came, and were ready to join the others at the ceremony and enjoy the wedding feast together with their community.

This story is specifically a metaphor for being prepared for Christ's second coming, but I believe it also applies to our lives in general when it comes to being prepared for the sake of the Gospel. If, like the wise virgins, we lived in such a way that we were prepared for our communities' worst-case scenarios, how much more often would we be able to serve others? What if we kept our cars filled with gas just in case a friend needed to borrow it? What if we worked hard to keep a little extra money in our savings account just in case someone we knew was short on rent that month?

The point is to live ready and available, because believers (and nonbelievers) will call on us for help from time to time, and we won't necessarily be able to anticipate it. Can you remember a time when your car broke down and you had to call a friend to pick you up on the side of the road? How relieved did you feel when that friend was available to come get you at a moment's notice? I bet you remember that friend and still appreciate their willingness to come to your aid when you needed it. In the same way, we can be a supportive community for believers so that (a) we can support each other in times of need, and (b) nonbelievers will look at us and think, "How do they live like that? I'd like to live like that, too." We can also be available to serve nonbelievers and snatch up opportunities to love them like Christ would in the moment.

What are you doing as a couple to keep your lamps lit, for each other and for members of your community? How can you use your time together to prepare for future times of trouble?

PRAYER

Ask that God would enable you to prepare your lives so that you're ready and available for others.

Ask God to open your eyes to opportunities for you to jump in and serve where help is needed.

Ask that God would enable you to hold your time and possessions with an open hand and be willing to use them in ways that serve others.

Serving One Another

For you were called to freedom, brothers. Only do not use your freedom as an opportunity for the flesh, but through love serve one another. For the whole law is fulfilled in one word: "You shall love your neighbor as yourself."

—

Galatians 5:13–14

Early in your relationship, you may be excited for and love the opportunity to serve your significant other. You might feel great happiness cooking them dinner or surprising them with an outing to their favorite restaurant. You might feel like you're practicing doing life together if you self-sacrificially tidy up after them or drive them to work or class.

But as much as you might feel like doing these nice things now, there will probably come a day when you don't. That doesn't mean that feeling goes away permanently, but somewhere along the line, life starts to happen. As you grow more comfortable in your relationship, the need to make grand and remarkable gestures becomes less and less of a priority. You'll be pulled in so many directions by work, volunteer activities, maybe kids someday—after all that, will you still feel like helping your significant other with their laundry? Running errands for them? Doing things for them that aren't really your responsibility?

Since Josh's primary love language is quality time and mine is acts of service, you can imagine how the daily workload used to divide itself early on in our relationship. After we had been dating for a couple of years, Josh would come over and visit the home where I was living with several other women and make himself at home, grabbing a bowl of cereal to eat and sitting on the couch to hang out with everyone. Once, I had just finished doing everyone's dishes when Josh came into the kitchen and placed his dirty bowl in the sink rather than the dishwasher, which was open right beside me. *What on earth?* I thought. *How could he be either so ignorant or so entitled?* I immediately felt anger and resentment, so much so that, without realizing it, I began grumbling to myself—I wasn't speaking out loud, but my mouth was definitely moving.

Unfortunately, Josh observed this from the other room and asked, "Uh, you okay, Chels?" I was immediately horrified and embarrassed —both at my bad attitude and the fact that I had been semi-unconsciously pretend-scolding Josh. My embarrassment put my heart in check right away. Sure, what Josh did wasn't very considerate, but how much worse was my instant attitude compared to something he had simply over-looked? I didn't for a second stop to give him the benefit of the doubt, communicate that I'd like him to put the bowl in the dishwasher, or simply want to serve my significant other by cleaning his dish.

While this incident has stuck with me over the years, it's been a long lesson for Josh, too. There have been other times in our relation-ship when he's had feelings of resentment because of things he had to do for me that he initially felt weren't *his* responsibility. It's safe to say that at some point in your future, you and your significant other will have to pick up each other's slack. While it's important to be honest with them when you feel they could realistically be doing better, the line dividing our responsibilities from our partner's ebbs and flows; it's hardly ever fifty-fifty.

As I mentioned, early on in your relationship, you may feel more excited at the chance to show your partner your willingness to serve them. It comes much more naturally when we're in the early, blissful stages of the relationship and we want to impress our partner, to show them how great a partner we can be. But how much *more* beautiful is the idea of serving someone when it's inconvenient, when impressing them is no longer vital to your relationship?

When you've cemented your relationship with your significant other, you may feel much more inclined to hold them accountable for "their share" of the work. When Josh and I start to feel this way about each other, we try to remember that Christ constantly makes up for "my share" and "his share" of the relationship. Christ loved us before we were ever able to love Him back. "For if while we were enemies we were reconciled to God by the death of his Son, much more, now that we are reconciled, shall we be saved by his life" (Romans 5:10). And in our relationship with Christ, we constantly fail to love Him like He deserves and serve Him in the way He calls us to. We constantly need His grace and forgiveness in order to help us be people who act as though Christ is everything. Because He is! But we often forget that when life gets busy or hard. Taking time every day to reflect on God's grace will help us have a godly perspective of the times when we must do more than our share of the work in our relationships.

PRAYER

Ask God to keep your heart humble and to help you always remember how much we are in desperate need of His own grace.

Ask God to help you be long-suffering and patient when it comes to serving your significant other.

Ask God to help you find joy in self-sacrificial service to anyone, including your significant other.

Living Life in Sync

Complete my joy by being of the same mind, having the same love, being in full accord and of one mind.

—

Philippians 2:2

It's a stereotype that relationship books focus on communication, isn't it? Well, let's be stereotypical today. Throughout your dating relationship, and if/when you and your partner get married, you're going to need to learn how to effectively communicate. I've found that the older a couple is when they get together—or, more realistically, how *independent* they individually are—the more they struggle to learn to do this effectively. That isn't a bad thing at all! Being independent is a great skill to have mastered when you enter into a relationship. It can just be hard to blend your independence with another individual's independence.

I had a conversation with a marriage counselor in training. He was single and had never been married, and he told me he believed every single relationship issue ultimately boiled down to bad communication. To be honest, I have to disagree. Yes, bad communication does lead to a lot of issues and has its own consequences, but is it the reason for *every* issue in relationships? Not hardly. What about selfishness? Addictive tendencies? Bitterness? Ultimately, becoming dead to ourselves and alive in Christ is the only true healer of our relationship problems. However, communication *is* often the key to helping you and your significant other work through many of these issues together, as well as navigate your day-to-day lives.

I learned a valuable lesson about communication when I started working remotely for a company in New York City. You would think that since I live on the West Coast, we might have difficulties working together on many different projects on a daily basis. However, one thing that my team does very efficiently is communicate. We meet regularly and keep in constant contact via messaging and e-mail. Although I've never set foot in the New York office, I feel as if I know each individual I work with and am in fluid communication with them at all times.

I like to think of communication in a romantic relationship as something like that: constantly working to stay in sync. As you grow in your relationship with each other, this will become more and more important. For example, when you first start dating your significant other, the need to talk about finances isn't too important, but as you get closer to possibly entering into a marriage together, communicating about finances becomes absolutely necessary.

The best and most practical way a couple can stay in sync is by asking each other questions. For example, if a friend asks if you and your partner can hang out Friday night, don't simply say, "Yes, we're free!" Check with your partner first. They may already have plans, and your assumption that you can dictate their schedule might lead to disappointment and hurt feelings.

Of course, there are ways to stay in sync other than simply communicating your plans. By spending time in the Word and in prayer, both individually and together, you will come to find that the more your mind-sets are aligned with Christ, the more they're aligned with each other. When you hear of a family in need at church, the Holy Spirit may first speak to you both individually about helping that family. Then, when you discuss it together, you'll already be on the same page in your desire to jump in and help.

Being in sync also helps during times when you disagree. Although you may feel differently about something, like your availability to hang out with your friend on Friday night or your ability to help a family in need, being in sync will allow you to understand your significant other's reasons for disagreeing. In that case, even though you may disagree, because you're in sync you'll be able to at least respect your significant other's reasoning.

PRAYER

Ask God to remind you to take your thoughts and concerns first to Him and then to your significant other.

Ask that God would allow you and your partner to communicate in a way that both shows respect and assumes the best of your partner.

Ask that God would help you and your significant other align with Him above all else and, as a result, align with each other.

How to Change Your Partner (Hint: You Can't)

Do not be conformed to this world, but be transformed by the renewal of your mind, that by testing you may discern what is the will of God, what is good and acceptable and perfect.

—

Romans 12:2

This week I want to discuss something we've all done, something that's necessary to address in a book like this: anticipating change from your significant other. Have you ever entered into a relationship looking at the *potential* of the person you were dating rather than the reality? I know I have. Several times. I would take a look at some of the basic characteristics of the person I wanted to date and envision who they might be one day if they were to stop being selfish or sexually immoral or whatever else. The thing is, I almost never saw this change happen. The person I started dating was the same exact person the day we broke up. And why did we break up? Because of the same characteristics I had hoped would change when we started dating.

How many movies and TV shows portray a couple who come so close to breaking up, but then one of them gives the other a talk or an ultimatum, and that person is so inspired that they go through a complete life change, solving all the couple's problems? In my experience, women have this fantasy more often than men, but both genders are guilty of it. When we're attracted to someone, we often think that means we must also be compatible with them, or we make excuses for them in order to overlook certain less than ideal characteristics. Sure, she might make you laugh, but is she completely selfish most of the time? Or you might love the fact that he helps when your car or your kitchen sink needs repair, but does he make excuses to avoid spending quality time with you?

As much as you might like your significant other to change, people don't alter their core characteristics just because someone asked them to. Even if they try for a little while, there's a huge likelihood that those characteristics will continue to show up time after time. Truthfully, people tend to change only when they're uncomfortable with the way things are now and when they can see their own role in that discomfort. That's why it's extremely important to have a realistic and complete picture of the person you're dating. If you expect them to simply step up or become more mature one day, well . . . don't.

So what's a person to do if they find something frustrating about their significant other's personality?

First, put it in perspective. Is this characteristic a big red flag? Is this something you think you could live with for the next 50-plus years if your partner never improves in this area? Is it something you merely find annoying, or is it sinful in the eyes of God?

Having a realistic view of your significant other involves asking yourself these kinds of questions and thinking critically. While the idea of thinking critically about your partner might not sound very nice, and while I do encourage looking at them with grace and humility, it's important to have a realistic idea of the person you're committing to a relationship with, and it's better to do that now rather than after you get married. Once you're married, those characteristics you found frustrating while you were dating will still be there, but now you'll have to learn to live with them.

So take time to observe your significant other. How do they act around and relate to others? Do they pursue a one-on-one relationship with Christ without your encouragement to do so? When speaking with others, do they usually bring the conversation back to talking about themselves, or do they show an interest in the person they're speaking with?

None of this is intended to scare you out of being in a relationship. No one is perfect, and if you spend your days waiting for Mr. or Ms. Right to come along, you'll be waiting a long time. The most important piece of advice I can give is this: Find someone who shows evidence of being convicted and changed by the Holy Spirit. They may have weird quirks or somewhat annoying personality traits, but if they truly love the Lord and have a humble spirit, they will be the type of person who is willing to change when God's Word calls for it. Beyond that, when two people have the common goal of working toward a relationship that is glorifying to God, the Holy Spirit makes it possible for very different people to come together and live in harmony with each other. Find a partner who is humble and willing to admit when they're wrong, loves the Lord, and (on their own) constantly works toward being more Christlike, and the question of whether they'll change some large aspect of their personality may well become moot.

PRAYER

Ask God to help you be the type of person who strives to glorify God and is willing to change to achieve that.

Ask God to help you think critically of your significant other for you, so you're relying on His judgment instead of yours.

Pray for your significant other that God would continue to grow them and use them for His will.

What God Has Joined Together

The disciples said to him, "If such is the case of a man with his wife, it is better not to marry."

—

Matthew 19:10

Sometime after Josh and I first got engaged, I took a long walk with his family. During this walk, his dad, Dave, told me the story of how he met Josh's mom, Camille.

Dave was told by a friend that there was a young, single Christian woman. What the friend didn't tell him was that she was a single mom of two young girls. On their second date, Camille told Dave that she was a mom. Being just out of college and having never been a parent before, Dave decided it would be best for him to move on.

But a month or two went by, and God began to speak to my father-in-law's heart. He began to feel convicted. He thought, *If I, a Christian man, won't give this woman and her daughters a chance, then who will?* He decided to pursue Camille again, knowing full well what he might be getting into. Hardly a year later, they were married, and Dave was immediately both a husband and a father of two.

Needless to say, they had their struggles when adjusting to their new lives together. Remember, Dave was fresh out of college. He was also starting his own physical therapy practice and was extremely involved in ministries at their church. Camille, meanwhile, was used to the life of a single mom, working multiple jobs to support her kids. Early on in their marriage, they had a lot of financial strain, and for a while, they really had to focus on determining how life would work *together* when they were each used to being independent.

Throughout this time, no matter how many fights they got into or what kind of struggles they went through, they understood that there was no backing out. When they said their marriage vows, they had made the choice to enter into a covenant before God that could not be broken. That being the case, Josh's parents had decided together that they would never bring up the topic of divorce. Since they knew that their marriage was a lifelong commitment, the topic of divorce was simply off the table. Even bringing it up flippantly or sarcastically during a fight wasn't acceptable.

Since they both agreed that the decision they made was for life, when their marriage hit its low points, they understood that if they didn't seek help and improve, they were going to be unhappy for a very long time. So they made improving themselves and working on their marriage a priority. Even today, after more than 25 years of marriage, Josh's parents still regularly retreat to have time alone together. They attend marriage conferences and read godly books together in a constant effort to grow more spiritually mature and have a more Christ-glorifying marriage.

The verse at the beginning of this week's devotion is a reaction from Jesus's disciples when He talks about marriage and divorce, saying, "So they are no longer two but one flesh. What therefore God has joined together, let not man separate" (Matthew 19:6). It was a hard message for the disciples to hear, as you can see from their response. They thought maybe if there was no possibility of divorce then it would be better not to get married at all—such was the gravity of making an oath before God that was meant to last a lifetime. They understood how difficult it would be to maintain a relationship for years and years on end. Even so, God chose to model marriage after the relationship He would have with His church: one that models reconciliation, restoration, and joy. And throughout His Word, He teaches Christians over and over again how to live peacefully with one another, whether they're married to each other or not.

I tell you this because I want you to have a sober and realistic view of marriage. One day, the excitement of living together and doing life together will wear off. But marriage can still be ever so purposeful and filled with joy if we allow Christ to shape us into figures that look more and more like Him. If marriage is a true picture of the self-sacrificial and forgiving love that Christ showed us, that means it's one of the most beautiful ways in which we can show Christ to the rest of the world.

Take some time to privately consider and pray about the permanence of marriage and the oath you hope to one day make before God. Then come together and talk about how serious you are about the words Jesus said, and what that will mean if and when you come face-to-face with difficult times in your future marriage. Discuss together what you plan to do if you feel like your marriage is really struggling. What will it take for you to seek prayer and advice from friends, family, or members of your church? At what point will you go to counseling? Will you ever bring up divorce? Discuss these things together and come up with your own disaster plan before you ever need it. Of course, ideally, you won't need it. But what will it hurt if one day your marriage seems to be struggling and you've already agreed on a plan to fix it?

PRAYER

Ask God to help both you and your partner have a sober and realistic view of marriage.

Ask God to prepare you both now for a God-glorifying marriage in the future.

Ask that God would always give you the love and desire to forgive each other and work through your differences in order to have a relationship that reflects His own love and forgiveness.

Appendix: 12 Date Ideas

The 12 date ideas I suggest below are intended to help you and your partner learn more about each other, bond, and give you something fun to do to make memories together. Any couple, anywhere, should be able to enjoy these—but put your own spin on each one. Plan special time with your partner once a month to give these ideas a try, in addition to working through the devotional. It's always easy to plan a trip to the movies, but it's nice to have a few new and interesting ideas tucked up your sleeve. Bring a camera to record the memories, and remember to dive deeper together!

1. **Go kayaking or canoeing.** There's just something about being near the water that makes the world look a little bigger and ourselves look a little smaller. Grab your boyfriend or girlfriend and head down to your favorite body of water (perhaps you live in a place where you have easy access to a local lake or river) and rent canoes or kayaks for a couple of hours. Take it slow as you explore and see what new conversation topics naturally come up as you're paddling along.

2. **Plan a picnic.** An outdoor picnic with your significant other may seem old-fashioned, but put a little personal spin on this date by challenging each other to make a dish that will surprise the other. You might get to learn something new if you've never made the dish before, your significant other may learn something new about you, and you may be impressed with each other's cooking skills. Don't forget the sparkling cider and a warm blanket.

3. **Attend a local fair or festival.** Festivals and fairs are great for three reasons: people watching, amazing food, and

way-out-of-the-ordinary experiences. Experience them together with your significant other. Each of you can make a list of your top three things you want to do at the fair or festival and enjoy them one by one together. Make it a point to try some unusual fair food (fried candy bars, anyone?).

4. **Get dressed up and take in some culture.** Even the staunchest jeans-and-T-shirt folks have to dress up once in a while. Even though the days of school dances are behind you, take an evening to look sharp. Go browse an art gallery or visit a local art museum, or attend the ballet, orchestra, or opera. Take in some culture in your Sunday best, and really take in the art or exhibits, then be sure to discuss.

5. **Indulge in a nice dinner.** Hey, that burger place around the corner will always be there. This weekend, search for or ask around for recommendations of some of the best places to eat in a metro area near you. Then take the afternoon to walk around the city and finish the night eating at a fancy-pants restaurant. If funds are tight, consider staying in and cooking dinner together.

6. **See a drive-in movie.** Talk about nostalgia! All you need for this date night to be magical is a car and a blanket. With a little bit of searching, you can find old-fashioned drive-ins around many metro areas. Grab some popcorn and snacks, open up the back hatch or plant yourself on the roof of the car, and enjoy a night taken from a scene of your childhood, with your best person.

7. **Watch the sun rise.** This date is for the early risers! If there's good hiking around where you live, go to bed early the night before, dress warm, and bring a flashlight. When you reach the top of the trail, pause to watch the sunrise. You might want to pack a blanket and a few snacks to enjoy for breakfast on your hike.

8. **Attend a baseball game.** Baseball games are great date opportunities because they afford conversation *and* entertainment, unlike a trip to the movies. Even if you're not a fanatic, baseball games are fun for everyone—there's stadium food, getting dressed up in game day attire, and watching the entertainment between innings. Of course, going to the ballpark is also great if you love baseball, too.

9. **Take a class together.** It's time to try something new. Whether it's cooking, martial arts, or salsa dancing, learning something new with your boyfriend or girlfriend can be bonding and useful. This also makes for a great repeat date, and both you and your significant other can take turns choosing the classes that appeal to you most.

10. **Have a board game night.** Board game nights make for perfect date nights. This is a great exercise in learning how each other thinks as well as certain things about your personalities. Each of you should pick your favorite board game. Did your significant other choose a game that requires thinking and strategy? Or a game that requires the players to act out a scene? It might be fun to pick up a new game neither of you have played and try something different.

11. **Test your strength at a rock-climbing gym.** This date at useful for exercising those forearms and shoulders as well as bonding with your significant other. While you climb, they'll be able to guide you to the best places to put your hands and feet while you ascend to the top of the wall. Once you've had enough practice, why not take this date to the great outdoors and practice on some real rocks?

12. **Taste test your local coffee shops.** Every town has at least a couple of coffee shops and cafés. Why not put them to the test by creating your own scorecard and taste testing the same latte at each place? Rate each latte by characteristics like foaminess, flavor, sweetness, etc. After the date, you'll have determined your new go-to place for coffee dates.

References

Chapman, Gary. *The 5 Love Languages: The Secret to Love That Lasts*. Chicago: Northfield Publishing, 1992.

Warren, Rick. *The Purpose Driven Life*. Grand Rapids, Michigan: Zondervan, 2002.

Verses Index

Index

Acknowledgments

Thank you from the bottom of my heart to Nana, my editor. I'm sure I had you pulling your hair out some days, but you stuck with me and kept me on track! There would be no book without you. Along with that, I want to thank all the other teams who worked on this devotional to make it come to life.

Thank you to my husband, Josh, for giving me something to write about. Also, you're great.

Thank you to my parents, Lee and Sue, and Josh's parents, Dave and Camille, for sharing their own stories and advice throughout our lives. Thank you also for your prayers and support.

Thank you to Gospel Community Rivermont, our church in Lynchburg, Virginia, where we truly learned what it means to live in Christ-centered community.

To John Piper, who will always be an inspiration to me.

To my kids, David and Evy, who have taught me to be self-sacrificing and see the world with an open heart.

About the Author

Chelsea is the owner and creator of the blog, *Living the Sweet Wife*, where over 100,000 people read her advice on marriage and family each month. She also works as a content marketer for the New York City tech start-up Scouted. She, her husband, Josh, and their two children spend their time looking for new places to hike and explore beautiful Washington State. Chelsea and Josh met while attending Liberty University, where they grew in their faith and dated for three years. They were married on the windy coast of Washington in 2013. Six months later they found out they were pregnant with their son. Throughout their dating and marriage relationship and into parenthood, they've been learning what it means to live loving God and loving others in a self-love world. For advice on marriage and family, read her blog (ChelseaDamon.com) or follow Chelsea and her family on Instagram @chelsealeighdamon.